HOW NOT TO BE GOOD

The A to Z of Anxiety:

a memoir in just over 26 parts

Elli Johnson

WORDSCAPE

How Not To Be Good
The A to Z of Anxiety: a memoir in just over 26 parts.

Written by Elli Johnson
Edited by Fiona Shaw
Design by Emma Jones
Proofreading by Lucy Chesters

Printed and bound in the UK by Resolution Print Management

ISBN: 978-1-9160267-0-4

First published in March 2019 by Wordscape Ltd.
The Mezzanine, Northern Lights Building, 5 Mann Street
Liverpool L8 5AF
wordscape.org.uk

For Matt.

Contents

Contents

This is a story
about me.

About who I was before;
how at 30 I was diagnosed
with anxiety and
depression; what I did about
it; and who I am now.

It's a story about someone
waking up and taking
charge of their life.

I'm reading in the bath
when I come across a
sentence so honest it leaps
off the page. The only
response is to stop, put the
book down, close my eyes
and sink a little lower into
the water. The words float
toward me.

> Anne Lamott:
> *"What I wanted my
> whole life was relief."* [1]

What I wanted my whole life was relief.

And this is where my story must start,
with this longing for relief.

With desperation.

It is 2009, two weeks before my 30th birthday. I'm sitting on the sofa when my husband, Matt, hands me an envelope. In it, a letter describes the birthday celebrations he has planned for me. He had wanted to make the whole thing a surprise, but knows I find this hard. He has organised a party for me at a bar in town and booked us into a smart hotel for the night. My parents are going to look after our three children, to give me a break and enable me to enjoy myself.

I am grateful. He has tried hard to construct an event I could enjoy. He has answered all the questions (and objections) he knew I would have. But even with this degree of preparation and thoughtfulness, my stomach sinks. How will I tell him it is impossible?

I say I can't have a night away from our baby. I say the feeding and expressing would be too tricky. I say I would be uncomfortable and unable to relax. I know he can see through my thin excuse. He's annoyed, disappointed. I talk fast, trying to make it sound reasonable, hoping he doesn't see me as controlling and ungrateful.

I don't tell him the real reason: it is all too much and I am terrified.

Rewind one month and we're in France with some of our closest friends.

> That year my husband, with an air of defeat, had said: *"You choose. You decide what you want to do on holiday. Make it a holiday you want to go on. I can never get it right, so you pick."*

1. p.11 from *Help, Thanks, Wow*; Anne Lamott

So I chose a holiday as safe and stress-free as possible.

A house in the Dordogne in France with a pool. Enough room for everyone. Peaceful. Where no one would ask anything of me and we could stay at the house and not go anywhere – save the supermarket – if we wanted.

And for a while, I'm okay. I cope with the heat and the breastfeeding and the broken nights to be expected when holidaying with a tiny baby. We relax and have fun, enjoying days splashing about with the kids in the pool and evenings sitting out under the stars drinking cheap red wine.

One evening we decide to go to a nearby market for dinner. Trestle tables fill the square. We wander, admiring the stalls selling hot food. A local band plays on the makeshift stage. Children dance while the adults sit watching and smiling, drink in hand.

Then, unexpectedly, our friend's child is ill. They quickly leave to go back to the house. And suddenly, out of nowhere, I am plunged head first into an all-consuming fear.

Wave after wave of terror floods my body.
My heart pounds.
I shake.
My temperature rises.
I want to flee, to run away.
I am undone.
I cannot think in a straight line.
My thoughts swirl and attack me.

I push the buggy over cobbled streets. I think if I am moving, maybe I can distract myself from the impending disaster which draws me ever closer. I am looking for a way out, respite, relief. I cannot find it.
I am overwhelmed.

My husband watches me. He sees me disappearing, recognising the warning signs he has become all too familiar with. He tries to calm me, tries not to become angry at how my inability to control myself is derailing another evening. I take deep breaths and focus on my children playing nearby. But I can't quiet my mind.
I am plummeting head first, hell-for-leather, to the pit of fear and shame that lives inside of me.
Unable to focus on anything, I am consumed with what is happening in my body and mind. I try to catch my breath, to stop my stomach churning.

We walk to the car. I pretend I am okay.
I bite my lower lip hard, tasting blood.
Anything to pull me out of the inner turmoil.

We drive home, cutting short our evening out. I look out over the fields of sunflowers, heads bowed as dusk approaches. I watch the sun set and feel like a fool. Surrounded by all this beauty but unable to enjoy it.

I cry. I try to hide it, but I can't.
I weep with desperation.
All I wanted my whole life was relief.

is for Anxiety

In the autumn of 2009, shortly after the birth of our third child, I am diagnosed with post-natal depression and anxiety.

I'd heard of post-natal depression: the Baby Blues, a leaflet in the doctor's office, a story in a TV drama. I had anecdotal information about that.

But anxiety? What was that? I had no idea.

It seemed like a made-up condition. Something the generation before me would call a 'modern phenomena'. Which, I'm pretty sure, is code for, 'you aren't as tough as we are and need to pull yourself together.'

If I'd said I 'suffered with anxiety' ten years ago, eyebrows would have raised. It would have been like saying I suffered with excitement or anticipation.

Dealing with anxiety is not the same as being nervous.
I feel nervous before an exam, or job interview because
there is a reason to be (I might fail, they might not like me).
Nerves force me to prepare, they stop me being complacent.
They have a purpose. Once the event is over the feelings
subside, the reason for them gone.

But when you suffer with anxiety (or Generalised Anxiety
Disorder, as it's sometimes called) the feeling never subsides,
not completely.

It is a mental illness.

(Which is a phrase I have had to practise saying out loud, to
make it less scary. These are hard words to own).
The internal response that once alerted me at times of
danger, is stuck in the 'ON' position. Safe environments and
activities feel threatening. The low level hum of anxiety
becomes the ever-present soundtrack to my life. I waste
huge amounts of energy trying to look 'normal'; to appear as
though I am not over-analysing Every Single Thing.

I spent much of my twenties trying to suppress the
eruptions that occurred when anxiety completely
overwhelmed me. It took me ten terrifying years to learn
the correct name for these experiences: panic attacks.

I didn't know I was ill.

I thought I was weak, it was all my fault and, if I was
stronger and tried harder, I wouldn't feel like this.

The shame that accompanied these feelings
stopped me seeking help.

For me anxiety came coupled with depression; they were a pair. I would fluctuate between the exhaustion and despair depression brought, and the adrenalin which flooded my body when anxiety took charge.

After a couple of years the depression lifted. But anxiety was more difficult to shift. I was circling a whirlpool, walking around the edge, trying not to look into its waters for fear of losing balance and being consumed. I looked at others going about their everyday lives and wondered how it was possible to live so free.

Managing the anxiety in my life took all my energy.
It tied me in knots.

It paralysed me.

B IS FOR
BEFORE
WE BEGIN

It is a hot day so my editor suggests we meet in a café out of the sun. The tables and chairs resemble old school furniture. I sip a ginger beer and wait for her to deliver the feedback. What needed re-writing or clarifying, what could be improved? Our conversation was helpful, positive.

We reach the end of our discussion and she looks down, concern momentarily crossing across her face.

She pauses and says quietly:
"There is one other thing. One note I wanted to deliver face-to-face – I wasn't sure how you would receive it in an email. I wanted to say something your friends won't say, but something I am sure you will hear once you publish this."
"Yes?" I waited.
"I just wanted to warn you.
Some people will probably tell you this is self-indulgent."

She winced.
I smiled.

Of course some people will think this is self-indulgent.
Her words don't phase me.

I've spent years wrestling and making peace with this thought. While writing this book, I've questioned many times if I should continue. My words have felt insignificant, my story unremarkable. I've worried my pain was not dark enough, tragic enough, extreme enough, to justify filling these pages. What right did I have to tell my story, to write about my experiences?

I am fortunate. I have a family who love me, a house to work in. I have a therapist I trust who I can see when I need to. I don't have to hold down multiple jobs to cover the basic costs of living. My children are healthy and happy.
If I had real problems I'd know about it, right?
I've been down this rabbit hole of squirmy comparison many, many times. Every time when I have finally aired, I am convinced of two things.

1. I can only write my story as truthfully as possible.

And,

2. Pain is pain is pain.

This is my story.

How it happened, what I did next, what I learnt.
This is how it unfolded for me.

I can't make generalisations.
There is no 'one size fits all' set of symptoms and solutions.

But I've realised that – just because your experience is different to mine – it doesn't make mine irrelevant. In fact, it's only when we all become brave enough to share our stories and talk about our truths that we will see we're not alone.

And pain is pain is pain.

Just because your pain might be more brutal or devastating than mine does not stop mine hurting. Just because my anxiety, my panic attacks, may be more visceral than yours doesn't mean yours aren't causing you anguish.

Trying to compare one person's suffering with another is never helpful. This perspective kept me trapped, it delayed me finding the help I needed. I had friends whose stories seemed to show suffering far greater than mine; who had lost loved ones suddenly, who were living with chronic illness, who were battling infertility.

My story of suffering felt slight in comparison. I didn't think my experiences justified time and energy spent on them, so I let the situation continue unchecked for many years. Years when I could have been learning and growing and healing, I spent feeling like a failure because my problems weren't as bad as the next person's.

What a waste of time.

I know some people reading this will have experienced far worse than me. (I'm so sorry.)
And others will have found support quicker and learnt faster how to help themselves.
In a world where we feel the need to measure every damn thing, let's not measure our pain.
It is irrelevant and unhelpful.

All our stories matter.
My story and your story and everyone else's story.

B is for Breakdown

Sometimes a breakdown happens suddenly: an irrevocable crash, smashing life as you knew it to pieces. Sometimes it happens slowly. Piece by piece. You break apart until you are unrecognisable.

It is our tenth wedding anniversary. We have stolen away to a hotel in Majorca for a few nights without the children. The walls are whitewashed and the water clear. To be well enough to be here feels like a triumph. I am one year post-diagnosis and doing better. We lie by the pool. I read and he listens to music. We sleep. We take stock.

Over dinner we talk without the interruption of children or the background noise of the washing machine. We begin to process how the last year has been.

After some time, my husband tells me he thinks I have been ill for a long time – maybe most of our married life.

This silences me.
My stomach sinks.
I don't want to hear it.
I want him to be wrong.

I start to construct a defence against his argument but soon collapse to the inevitable truth in his words.

I feel like a fool.
And heartsick with regret.
All the wasted years.
Some people experience mental illness all-of-a-sudden.
Nothing, then everything. Calm, then storm.

Not me.

My breakdown did not hit like a speeding car, causing debris to fly and help to race toward me. There were no blue lights or get well soon cards. My breakdown happened incrementally so no one, least of all me, saw it happening. It was sinking sand into which I was trapped, sliding under inch by inch, month by month.

There was a me before all this happened.
A time before anxiety washed the colour from my life.

I had a happy childhood. Unusual, but happy. I was a talkative, energetic child. An outer-world person, always happiest with others; in a crowd, or sharing secrets with a close friend.

At 11, we moved from one port city (Bristol) to another (Liverpool). I found this adjustment difficult. I felt out of place, as though I didn't belong. At school I found the work easy but friends hard to come by. Instead, I discovered community among students in the growing church my parents had moved to Liverpool to start. (There's the unusual bit).

At 16 I changed school to attend the local Jewish high school. Here were my people – knee deep in staging theatre productions, furtively smoking just out of sight of the staff, taking trips to galleries to look at paintings and sculptures and going out dancing on a Saturday night. Here my enthusiasm and curiosity was not sneered at by my peers, but encouraged. I thrived. I went from here to study Drama at university in Liverpool, having already met (at church) the man I was going to marry.

We said "I do" in the summer after my first year at university. I was 20.

From then on, life became steadily busier. The plate of my life filled up with good things.

Marriage

a house

a degree

freelance work

a fledgling career

one child

then another

and another

church responsibilities

friends

Soon it was filled to over-flowing.
I had it all.

But, over time, I found I couldn't manage it all.

It became harder to make decisions.
I became reluctant to make plans.

I was no longer sure what I wanted.
I blamed the night feeds and the demands of pre-schoolers for my permanent exhaustion. I thought once I got through this phase – when that child was at nursery, when my husband's work load lightened, when I was no longer breast-feeding, or weaning, or potty training—then I would be back in control. I worked hard to maintain my ignorance. I convinced myself my feelings weren't a big deal and I would be turning a corner, soon.

Relief was just around the corner.   It had to be.

In the hurly-burly busyness of that time I didn't see how I was changing.

How it was affecting me; distorting any sense of who I was.

Leaving me with a hollowness at the core.

My mental health didn't fall apart overnight.

There was no one precipitating factor which made me ill; no one trauma that I could point to.

But I was drowning, sinking in a well of depression, suffocating with anxiety.

I
had
broken
down.

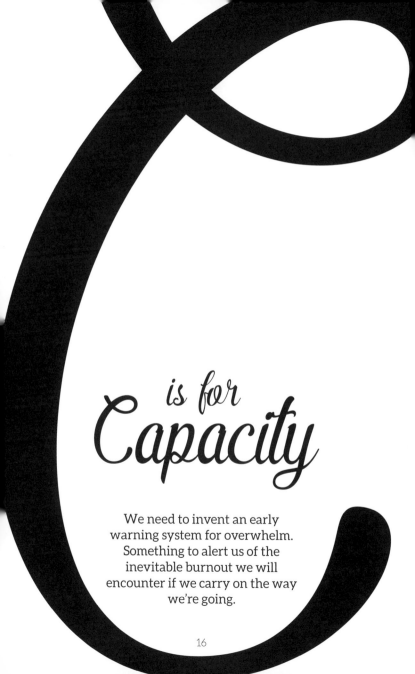

is for
Capacity

We need to invent an early warning system for overwhelm. Something to alert us of the inevitable burnout we will encounter if we carry on the way we're going.

In 2007, over red wine-fuelled late night conversations in the theatre bar, a writer friend and I dreamt up a theatre project. It evolved over the course of a year or two, in snatched hours between our paid work and on the rare occasions my two girls were otherwise occupied.

As the project reached its culmination, we assembled an excellent team: actors, an illustrator, a film maker and musicians. It was an ambitious project and entered the rehearsal phase three weeks after I'd given birth to our third child, our son, Ed.

Every morning, after dropping my girls at school and nursery, I drove into town, parked the car and carried the car seat up three flights of stairs to the rehearsal room. It was hot. The sun poured through the dusty windows which looked out over the rooftops of the city.

I lay Ed on a blanket on the floor, and attempted to focus on the work. I answered questions about style and structure and form and spoke to our brilliant musicians and illustrator. I thought about set and costume and how all the elements would come together on stage. I worked with the writer, tweaking the script, making changes, editing, refining. All the time trying to appear as though I was in control and coping well.

I wasn't.

My body felt awkward and ungainly, milk leaked through my top and my clothes didn't fit well. My brain was a soup. I was drained from the lack of sleep and the effort of trying to stay on top of everything: the production; practical arrangements for our family; the fear I wasn't doing a good job. I was skittish and inspiration was lacking.

I knew this production had potential, but was increasingly unsure I would be able to realise any of it.

I tried to shrug it off, to take it all in my stride.

I thought I would feel invincible, that this was how to have it all. Managing motherhood and creative work, budgets and schedules and packed lunches and homework.

> But it was hard.
> Really hard.

I tried to hold everything in my head, to organise and lead well. I dug deep and pressed in, determined to do a good job. I'd decided I was the kind of person who was capable of ticking all the boxes all the time.
I thought I had to be.

I was dropping balls, worrying about the impact on my family. I was trying to remember what we were having for tea, rushing back to pick the girls up from the childminder before bathing them and getting them into bed. I knew my attention wasn't fully in the production and I felt guilty. I knew my girls were being passed from pillar to post and I felt guilty. No one was getting my best. As I juggled, I struggled not to feel hard done by.

I blamed others for the life choices I was making. Blamed my husband for working too much and my parents for not being available enough to help me with the kids.
I thought I had no choice but to carry on with my exhausting, stressful life.

But I was creating my own conditions for misery.

Had I acknowledged I wasn't coping, I could have asked for help, or chosen an easier way. But this didn't fit with my idea of who I thought I should be, so I carried on.

I couldn't let go of the idea I should be able to do – and have – it all. I wanted to be the good example of a hard-working mother who tends to others, whose kids are brilliant and has a thriving career. I wanted to be a, 'I don't know how she does it' mum.

I was raised around people who work hard and go the extra mile, in an environment where a strong work ethic was paramount to success and respect. All my life I'd believed that being someone who gets through their to-do list and doesn't quit is the best way (maybe the only way), to live a worthwhile life. Hard work and dedication were of primary importance. The opposite of having a large capacity and doing-it-all, was not moderation and balance, it was laziness and self-absorption.

I had to keep going.
Quitting was not an option.

I had no idea my capacity was finite.

I'll say that again.

I had no idea my capacity was finite.
That eventually I would reach my limit.

I didn't know I'd get to a point where saying 'yes' to more would affect my mental health.
I thought I could keep stretching and the elastic would never ping back and smack me in the face.
Until it did.

How much should we do?
How much is possible?
How much is good for us?

No one teaches this in school.
No one equips us to make these decisions.
I thought more was always better. I was wrong.

C is also for Child of the '90s

I was born in 1979, blissfully ignorant of how fortunate I
was to have been born in this place at this time; naively
assuming everyone had education as standard, access to
health care, clean clothes and drinking water.
When I encountered the hard side of life – pain or war
or inequality – it was in the way kids are exposed to it,
through news reports and history lessons. Suffering seemed
far away or long ago. I was beautifully protected. I believed
the life I led was the norm and we (the world) would
continue to head in the right direction. Things would only
improve as we grew ever more enlightened.

If that was the backdrop of my childhood, in my teenage
years it was the ground we walked on.

I was a teenager of the '90s.
In my small corner of the world, opportunity was
everywhere. Whether it was the rise of Britpop, the
burgeoning British film industry or the international
attention the YBAs were gaining, I saw only possibility.

I was 17 when Tony Blair came to power, ending 18 years of
Conservative rule. When we were told 'things could only
get better', we believed it. The Spice Girls sang of girl power,
but we already knew we were equal to anyone. Equality of
sex and race seemed a foregone conclusion and I couldn't
see any way we would still be battling for equal pay or
representation in my adult life.

Life was there for the taking; I could do whatever I wanted to do, be whoever I wanted to be.

That was what I was told.   This was what I believed.

I was in the generation who would not have to struggle against the prejudices of old.

Exposure to such potential and positivity in my formative years meant I quickly learnt how to dream big. I thought I was too sophisticated to be naive about the reality of the world – I listened to grunge and indie music, wore my Doc Martens with pride and relished the idea of being different. But the message of the decade – that life was there for the taking and success was my right – had gotten under my skin.

It all seemed so positive, how could it be unhealthy?
How could it be wrong to think like this?
I'd been taught to raise the bar, to reach for the stars, to follow my dreams.

Anything else felt like settling, felt like failure.

I had no idea that by living with these expectations, I was setting myself up for a fall.

D IS FOR
DO YOU
LOVE ME YET?

I climbed the five steps to the office where our course tutors had desks piled high with papers. Walking past the photocopier, I sat on a chair behind the make-shift bookcase. I was looking for advice. My words tumbled out.

The actors in the performance I was directing weren't as committed as I needed – they didn't appear to respect me, or believe in my ability to draw the best from them. I was frustrated and not sure how to get them on side, to make them do what I said. I didn't want to be strict. I wanted us to have a good working relationship, for it to be a fun experience.

I wanted them to like me.

I chewed on my thumb nail and waited for a response. The chair swung round.

His face was serious but his eyes smiled at my naivety;
"Oh. I see… that's the problem: you want to be liked.
Well, you need to get over that straight away.
That will get in the way of everything."

A few years later, I'm driving my Mum Bus – the ubiquitous people carrier. My two girls are in the back, strapped into car seats. As we stop at the traffic lights I start the pep-talk. My eldest (who was about four at the time) could have recited it by heart she'd heard it so often. Had she been a little older she would probably have rolled her eyes.

"Okay girls, we're going to our friend's house, but remember we are their guests. And we are at their house.
When you're at someone else's house you play what they want to play. You do what they want to do.
The toys belong to them, so, if they want something you're playing with, you give it straight back.
I need you both to behave well and be polite."

To the untrained eye it may have looked as though I was teaching good manners. In reality, I was micro-managing my children. Trying to control them so they behaved how I wanted them to. Although I pretended it wasn't, this was an appearance game. I wanted them to be polite and kind so I was seen as a good Mother – so my friend thought my children were great and would invite us back. So we – I – would be liked.

This need to be liked was hard-wired into me. Ideas about being a good person by putting others first had stuck fast to my community-centric, extroverted personality. I worked to make sure everyone had a good opinion of me. I anticipated friends' needs, offering help before they'd realised they needed it, whether they wanted it or not. I loved to be in the middle of someone else's crisis. To be the saviour, the superhero. I wanted to be the one they 'couldn't have coped without'.

I acquiesced to friends' suggestions when arranging where to meet up with the kids or for coffee.

I didn't want to be pushy or hold the responsibility if it turned out to be a bad idea. When I fell out with someone, or felt a friend was cool with me, I went into overdrive to try and remedy the situation. I sent apologetic texts and flowers, before double checking we were okay with a follow up 'chatty' message the next day. All the while I was in agony, thinking they were inwardly rejecting me and I would end up all alone.

I was only okay so long as you were okay with me.

I was so deep into people pleasing – looking to others for affirmation and reassurance – it felt part of my essential nature.

It was who I was.
I couldn't see it was harmful.
I called it kindness or selflessness.
I called it generosity and preferring others.
I·couldn't see it was eroding me.

When you want to please people you'll do what they ask, even if you know it's no good for you.
When you want to please people you'll take on responsibility for burdens that are not yours to carry.
When you want to please people you'll wake up one day and realise you don't know who you are or what you think, because you're a hundred different things to a hundred different people.

I had set myself up. I was being who I thought I needed to be to be loved and accepted.
Looking to others to guarantee my self-worth was a dangerous game and it was exhausting.
I was putting myself under immense pressure but couldn't see it. I thought this was what life was like for everyone.

Dear Matt,

Falling in love with you was easy.
I fell hard, head over heels, completely.

In church. I'm sat with my sister Chloe somewhere near
the back. She whispers loudly about how bored and
hungover she is. I'm ignoring her, trying to listen. Even
then I am a holiness try-hard. We've brought sweets:
Tootie Frooties and Jelly Tots to share with the students
sat near us. Claire and Mark and James and you.

It was another two and half years before we kissed, in
your filthy student flat in the early hours of the morning.
We had left the party early to come to your flat to check
on your friend who had consumed too much vodka jelly. It
felt electric, despite the lingering smell of vomit. The next
day I called Chloe (now at university) to brag about what
had happened. She couldn't believe it, that I had managed
to kiss you!

She didn't know it was really the other way around.

I was in the final year of school, studying for my A Levels
and you were completing your degree. You lived in a flat at
the bottom of the road and when I turned up after school
with some excuse or other to see you, your flatmate would
call to you, "Matt, your school-girl's here". I was worried it
would put you off. It didn't.

You told me you loved me after three weeks.
I didn't stand a chance.

You were not who my parents would have chosen for me, but they grew to love you.

You were not who I thought I would end up with either; the artist living off thin air and hope in a dilapidated loft.

You were a graduate buying your first home and setting up a business. You wore cheap suits and cold-called your business into life, refusing to take no for an answer. You were tenacious and determined and ambitious.

I took a year out after school, earned some money and did some travelling, before moving out of home to begin my degree. But I was not independent for long. Despite my tutor taking me to one side to check I wasn't making a huge mistake, we were married at the end of my first year at university. To those who knew us it was inevitable.

We married in a friend-of-a-friends' back garden in a glorified scout tent. My mum prepared the food and her best friend made my dress. Your brother brought the wine, my dad married us. Friends and family gathered to celebrate with us.

We were young and in love, I'm not sure anybody could have stopped us.

E is for

Throughout the second half of my twenties, whenever someone asked how I was, I would inevitably answer, "fine, just really tired".

I put my exhaustion down to my stage of life, to the age of my children and the broken sleep, but it was more than that.

This pressure to perform and please had made me anxious.

The more anxious I felt, the more I tried to hide it.

Hiding is exhausting.

Exhaustion

I am someone who has a loud internal monologue that accompanies me about my day, every day. A voiceover letting me know how I am doing, whether I am meeting the mark, it comments on my actions, thoughts and feelings.

How do you feel?
Tired. Washed up. Grey.

Why?
I don't know. Life. Everything. The kids have been up in the
night and Maddy was off school again last week. She gets
run down so often. And Matt has a demanding new client
at work so he's been leaving early and home late. I'm letting
down friends and family and my career appears to have
completely stalled now.

Well, that would do it.
Yes, but it's more than that. I'm exhausted in my head. I
can't explain. I don't know how much longer I can carry on
like this, with all this.
Life. It's just too much.

Can you be more specific?
It's not one thing, but lots of little things. I don't enjoy
playing with my children. I find it boring. I'm a terrible
parent. There's the odd moment of unsurpassed joy, but
often it feels like a drag, I'm filling in the moments; counting
down the hours until bedtime; until In The Night Garden
and Iggle-piggle heads off with his red blanket. I try to be
good and not complain—but I catch myself complaining
often. If only it was just a little bit easier, if only Matt
worked shorter hours, if only I had someone to help me.
My other friends seem to be coping, and I get through the
day okay, but it's all a bit depressing; the same shit day after
day. The same chores and conversations and mealtimes. The
same washing up and wiping down counter tops, the same
tidying away of the same toys. I feel grey. Just shades of
grey. No colour left in me.

Okay so lots of people feel this way… Life is hard.
Why does that not make me feel better? And there's this
other thing…

Yes?
Terror.

Terror?
I feel it in my brain and then it travels quickly to my
stomach. My stomach races and reels. I feel sea sick stood
on dry ground. It swallows me up. I can't see the way ahead.
I feel prickles of heat all over my body. My cheeks go red.
My hands become clammy. I start looking for the nearest
bathroom.

Are you ill?
Yes.
No.
I don't know.
I'm scared.
I want everyone and everything to go away.
I just need a break.
Some peace and quiet.
Everyone to stop talking.

My friends were coping. Thriving even. Or so it seemed.

Succeeding at motherhood and forging careers. Enjoying being with their children, keeping their house clean and tidy and presenting a good image to the world. Organising their childcare and pursuing work. They appeared happy and content; to be managing life well. Meanwhile I was scrabbling around trying to make my life meet the mark. The unchecked things left on my to-do list grew daily.

I kept digging deeper. Turning over new leaves.
Making plans and resolutions to be a better version of me. This new me would eat better, exercise more, have more time for my children and keep her house cleaner. This me would work hard and be a better friend; more considerate and thoughtful, I would text and call and send cards in the post. Once a year, on holiday when I had a little time to think, I read books about people who achieved their goals and fulfilled their destiny. Who were productive and organised. I wrote lists of new disciplines, determined to put them in place when I got home.

I was physically exhausted from trying to keep all the balls in the air. But more than that, I was mentally and emotionally exhausted. At 29, I was barely keeping my head above the waters of my anxiety.

I was trying so hard not to be scared.
Not to drown.

I was sure I was the only one who felt like this.

So, despite my increasing anxiety – and the fact I ended most days feeling so tired I could barely hold a conversation

– I carried on.

F is for Fight or Flight

My body is a prophet.

The year after graduation I was employed to run workshops based on Tony Kushner's brilliant and devastating play, *Angels in America*. The play, set in the 1980s, is about AIDS in America. As well as being redemptive and beautiful it is, at times, hard to watch. Its depiction of the effects of illness – both on those suffering and those caring for them – is graphic and brutally honest.

My role in these workshops, run for university students, was to take extracts from the text and use them as a basis for discussion and performance.
I handed out short scenes and, with a little direction, the participating students got their part of the text 'on its feet'. In their faltering, and heart-breakingly vulnerable ways, they brought moments from this play to life.

In one workshop something happened I could not explain. The youth of the students – their optimism and innocence combined with the intense subject matter – became too much for me to cope with.

One minute I was sitting on the floor in a circle with the rest of the students, watching one of the tiny performances; the next something had triggered my anxiety and I was headed for panic central. Suddenly I was falling, down the rabbit hole, away from reality.

I felt myself spiralling, struggling to cope.

My temperature rose; I felt disconnected from my body, as though I was watching myself from the outside.

I took deep breaths and tried to focus. The room swam. I was scared.

I became light headed. I pinched my arm, trying to pull my focus back to the present moment.

My rational understanding, which would have pointed out that what I was watching wasn't real, it was just a couple of students acting, was overwhelmed.
I was powerless to stop it.

I must have managed to mutter some intelligent words as the workshop progressed as normal, but I was not okay. Something had gotten under my skin. Embedded itself in my brain.

There are moments from this workshop that, nearly 20 years later, I can remember frame by frame. I still have a physical response to them.

My gut lurches. The hairs on my arms stand on end.

I have to catch hold of my thoughts before they move, speeding away from me toward inevitable despair.
Fast-forward a couple of weeks.
I'm in my car, a hand-me-down green Citroën, poorly executing a three-point-turn in my parent's road.
Mid manoeuvre, I have to stop. My heart is racing.

The sound of blood is rushing in my ears and my stomach churns as my mind jump-cuts to one of the scenes in the workshop. I don't understand what is happening.
It is out of my control.

I try to wrestle my mind back to safer territory; the weather, the trees, the bloody car, but I can't. I'm being forced to watch this scene, over and over again. It is on permanent repeat. Eventually I park the car and get out. My knees are knocking, my breathing heavy. I struggle to stand, to lock the car. I lean against the roof and close my eyes, squeezing them tight, using all my energy to focus on something, anything, else.

After a few moments, which feel like hours, the feeling subsides, calm returns.

It would be a long time before I would recognise this was my first panic attack.

When the amygdala (the section of the brain responsible for fear and preparing us in case of an emergency) gets aroused, the body kicks into fight or flight mode. When you are well, this mechanism helps you deal with danger and stay safe. If I was about to be attacked by a bear, for example, I'd be very grateful for the surge of adrenalin the amygdala would release, enabling me to fight. (Or, more likely, take flight as quickly as possible.)

A problem occurs when the switch in your brain to assess danger is faulty and can be triggered for no good reason. (This is how I understand it. I'm no scientist.)

During my 20s this happened with increasing regularity.

This memory, of the suffering depicted in this extract of this play, was the first trigger. The first incident I remember to throw me into panic mode.

It was the first trigger, but definitely not the last.

I can't recall every attack but, as the years passed, they happened frequently enough for me to become afraid of the feeling returning.

Fear of the fear.

I forced myself not to dwell on these attacks or give them more headspace than necessary. I didn't understand what was happening to me, or that there was anything I could do about it. I had no alternative but to try to ignore these attacks. When I felt fear creeping up my neck – the prickles of sweat on my face, the pins and needles in my fingers and the familiar stomach swirling – I fought hard to control my body. Through willpower alone I tried to force it to submit.

When I was unable to, I believed it was because I hadn't been trying hard enough. I was weak.
I couldn't see these attacks were actually a consequence of how hard I had been trying.

It wasn't until many years later I understood I had created the perfect conditions for panic.

Eventually, a build-up of pressure has to be released.
In plate tectonics, this displays itself as an earthquake or tsunami. A technicolor display along a fault line.
Panic attacks were my earthquakes; the inevitable consequence of the pressure I put myself under.

My body was trying to tell me something.

Your life is not working.
You need to stop.
You can't carry on like this.
It's too much.

My body was a prophet. It was declaring the truth long before I was able to hear it.

G IS FOR GOOD

Where I'm from: Growing up, faith was
not something we did, it was who we were.

It affected everything, from the way we spent our money
and our time, to the way we behaved and operated as a
family. Ours was not a cold religious household, far from it.
Most days, extras gathered around the long pine table in our
kitchen to enjoy noisy meals. Faith was not a list of rules
and rituals, it was a culture of generosity and inclusion.

This was the lens through which I saw the world.
More than career or financial success, my church community
was the barometer I looked to for feedback.
It wasn't forced on me, and it didn't feel repressive.
I wanted to be a good Christian.

This started well.

As a child I was taught biblical ideas. These gave me a strong moral code which looked like good behaviour.
I thought this was what it meant to be a Christian: to serve and help and tick boxes. To put others first, be obedient and colour within the lines. To be good and polite and not complain. It seemed like a good way to live.

I learnt basic transactional truths.
You are kind: you will receive kindness.
You share: your friends will share with you.
You forgive: you will be forgiven.
As a teenager, these same ideas kept me away from danger.

On occasion, I felt myself grappling with the un-nuanced nature of these beliefs, debating an idea which didn't seem to fit my skin. But I was always compelled to revert back to what I knew, it felt safe.

I understood how to find love and acceptance in this system. I tried hard. I underlined verses in my Bible and went to meetings. I prayed regularly and felt guilty when I didn't. I acquired knowledge: what behaviour was appropriate; the right answers to questions; the correct way to live. I played by the rules and when I broke one I was filled with regret and shame. I was good.

What I didn't know was that these ideas needed to evolve in the light of adulthood. Life was complicated, my faith needed to mature for it to hold the tensions I discovered the older I got. This didn't happen. Instead I stuck to my guns, trying to squeeze my adult desires and questions into a childlike understanding.

I behaved like an oversized toddler, obeying rules that only worked when the everyday stresses of life weren't my concern.

I had children of my own; a mortgage; a husband – but I looked to simplistic ideas from my childhood to teach me how to live.

Everything was black and white – there was no place for colour, tone, or subtlety.

And definitely no room for grey.
These binary ideas about good and bad and right and wrong prevented me making decisions about my life.
(They also made me self-righteous and judgemental.)
I looked for any indication I was succeeding. Ticking the holy-Jo box, appeared to offer me that assurance.

> I held on to the transactional system:
> **hard work**
> ✝
> **good behaviour = acceptance**
> as though my life depended on it.

> It felt the safest place to be.

I clung to the idea that if I was good then God would bless me and I would be okay.

Although I knew it wasn't a very sophisticated way of seeing the world, I trusted God weighed my offerings.

My prayer; my generosity; how much I read the Bible; my ability to live out the fruits of the spirit; to see if I'd done enough.

> I pushed for perfection.
> Anything else felt like failure.

I believed if I managed to maintain this way of life, then I would get what I wanted, I would be well, I would be happy. I wanted cast iron guarantees.

The flip side of this was that when things went wrong, I believed it was because of some fault in me. It was my deficiency or weakness which meant I wasn't able to control my anxiety.

Some sin.
Some inconsistency.
Some lack of faith.

I did what I thought was the best thing in these circumstances, I ignored my reality. I pretended I wasn't always fighting feelings of guilt and shame. I refused to look at the darkness in my heart. At my disappointment and fear. At the unexplained crevasses that opened up in the solid ground of my mind, when I was least expecting it.

This was the truth I believed about who I was:
If I behaved and was obedient, I was worthy.
If I made mistakes, I was not.

All the pressure I felt through my twenties found its roots in this misaligned understanding. I believed in some way I was in control – actions had consequences, so I'd better make sure I was doing life right.

I had misunderstood the very heart of my faith. I believed it was my responsibility to make myself acceptable to God. God was like Father Christmas. He would put me on the good list, accept me and love me, but only if I worked hard enough and was good.

This was a heavy load.
And one I was never designed to carry.

H is for Hyper

As I neared the end of my twenties I was in a dark place.

The buzz of anxiety ever-present, the panic attacks frequent and paralysing. My sense of failure complete.

I sought any way to minimise and hide the impact of this fear tearing through my life. I tried to not step on the cracks or touch the current which would sound the alarm.

For me, sickness was the trigger point for panic. I was highly sensitive to the idea that I might become ill.

Paranoid. Obsessed.

This was the line of code which had been corrupted, from which my panic attacks would erupt.

To protect myself I tried to eliminate any talk of, or proximity to, illness. Which – with a young family as part of a large community – was impossible.
I was on high alert at all times.

My nerve endings exposed. They fizzed and crackled.

I required constant reassurance, asking my husband,
"Am I going to be ill? Do you feel okay? Do you think that food was cooked properly?"
He would snap, frustrated, not knowing why I'd become preoccupied with what we ate.

As this route to panic became well worn in my mind, an attack could be triggered by the tiniest suggestion. An overheard half-conversation in the school yard could send me spinning. It wasn't long before my ability to race to catastrophe didn't even need a trigger in the present moment, a memory could be enough. This is how good at anxiety I was.

Regardless of what knocked me down, once I was falling, the over-rehearsed thought process would start:
'I might get ill.'
'I probably will get ill.'
'In fact I feel ill already'
'That's my stomach churning. I'm sure I am going to be ill.'
('Don't be ridiculous, you are just hungry.')
'Well, if I'm hungry, why do I feel sick?'
And so on.

My brain would take me on a whistle-stop tour of the past few months. I would remember every person I'd been in

contact with who was, or could have been, ill. I would think of all the food I'd eaten that could have been past its best.
I imagined what it would be like when I was sick or lost control in front of everyone I knew and respected.
I pictured the horror, the embarrassment, the humiliation.

When I was dealing with acute anxiety my stomach would be in shreds (an affect of the adrenalin-induced by the fight or flight response), and I would find myself caught in a loop. Worrying I would be ill, making myself ill through anxiety; knowing in my heart it was my brain that caused this illness. Shame. Disappointment. Fear.

The backdrop to this was always self-loathing. I raged at myself, heaping criticism on my head. Frustrated at how ridiculous it seemed, how weak and pathetic I felt, how powerless I was to stop it. I didn't know there was any other way to deal with panic attacks, I thought they were something I could only control through sheer focus and determination.

So, I tried to figure out how to shield myself from anything that would trigger my panic.

I walked away if someone mentioned illness.
I would turn off the radio at the mention of the word cancer, Bird Flu, epidemic, Zika Virus, Norovirus.
If, on social media, I saw someone had been ill, I would scroll quickly past and make sure I didn't see them or any of their family for a few weeks.

I secretly quarantined people.

Sometimes I would try and be brave and listen to a news report, thinking I needed to toughen up. To become stronger through exposure to the things I feared most. But this didn't go well. It only gave my brain ammunition in the shape of words, images and stories, to replay when I started to feel out of control.

Soon most television became threatening. I couldn't predict what was going to be said or shown and became very selective about what I chose to watch. I boiled it down to *America's Next Top Model* and *Emmerdale*.

Eventually I stopped socialising, apart from with a few carefully selected friends. Being at home felt safer. I wanted to be in an environment where I could hide away and avoid potentially humiliating situations. Where I had access to a clean bathroom if I needed it and could take myself off to bed if necessary.

I made my life smaller.

I thought that if I could manage my days and the activities I took part in, if I could control every element of my life, my anxiety would not be awoken.

Plans made in a moment of optimism were hurriedly aborted as I felt the threat grow. I felt my friends becoming irritated with me and decided it was easier to not make plans. Better to be a reliable bore than to let people down.

I used the kids as an excuse.
I said 'I couldn't get a babysitter', or 'I was shattered' (both often true, but not the reason I was saying no).

I turned down work.
I narrowed the remit of my days.
And it worked.
Sort of.

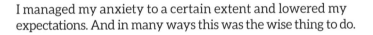

I managed my anxiety to a certain extent and lowered my expectations. And in many ways this was the wise thing to do.

But deep down I knew I didn't want the rest of my life to look like that. I was overwhelmed and dissatisfied, and my husband was growing more and more frustrated with me.

Where was the gregarious social animal he'd married?

Why was I continually exhausted?

Why did he have to spend so much time reassuring me about the craziness in my head?

I is for

I Can't Do It Any More

I had forgotten the person I used to be.
I was out of hope.

Change was not possible.

In September 2009 my husband insisted I get some help. After a lot of conversations and cajoling, I made an appointment to talk to a woman I knew vaguely, whose advice I had sought when I was looking for ways to help a grieving friend. We didn't use the word 'therapy', although she was a trained therapist and I was paying for her time.

I don't remember my first two sessions.
There were tears.

She was reassuring and I always came away feeling better, the load lifted, albeit temporarily.
It wasn't until our third session that the reality of the situation became clear.

I locked my car and crossed the road, thinking to myself: *'Okay, so, I might have to go and see someone. I'm obviously struggling and this is not good... but at least I've not got depression. At least I'm not on antidepressants. Now that would be hard to deal with. That would make me feel like a real failure...'*

It was only as I drove down the busy high street looking for a place to park that this had occurred to me. Comparing myself with others in what I deemed to be a worse situation made me feel better about my chaotic and emotional state.

Ugly but true.

The train of thought continued,
'Imagine being so weak you needed 'happy pills' to anaesthetise you. Only really flaky people need that. Thank God that isn't me. Thank God this is just a temporary circumstantial thing.'

I couldn't have admitted to thinking like this. Grace and compassion were important, and I knew my thoughts were not gracious, but this was what I thought.
What a lot of people think.

Ignorance creates a grace deficit.

Making my way across the road I rang the doorbell, arrogant assumptions neatly hidden. This time there was no small talk, no easing into the conversation. My therapist came straight to the point. She had been reviewing my notes and it had become obvious to her I was suffering with post-natal depression.

I burst into tears.
Through the next hour or so, she reassured me, explained how she knew, and described what it meant.

I felt scared.
What would this mean?
How would I cope?
What would people think?
How could I even begin to tell them?

But I also felt relief.
I had been holding on, holding it together for a long time and I was tired.

More than tired, I was exhausted.

I didn't know what was going to happen next, but I knew I could give up now. I could stop trying to save myself.

is for Just Let Go

I'd been white-knuckling it. Gripping tightly to the things I thought made a worthwhile life.

Slowly, I started to see I'd have to learn to unclench my fist.

My automatic response when life got tough was to double down and persevere. I knew the person I should be: strong, competent, popular, capable, and faith-filled.

I believed this was what success looked like. If I wasn't on this trajectory it was surely because I was weak and needed to try harder.

I didn't know it was possible to live another way.

The culture I was brought up in had been bombarding me with self-improvement plans and ideas about the kind of body, business, relationships, home and life I could have if I worked hard enough.

Church had been filling my head with stories of people who persevered and didn't quit or complain, regardless of the pain they were in.

It didn't matter if I looked to celebrity magazines or Bible studies to find my path, there was always someone promoting the idea that I could be a better version of me if only I put in the effort. There was always a new strategy, a new way to organise my time, a new parenting approach, a new way to make sure I prayed enough. I believed love and acceptance would be found by achieving and accumulating.

There was comfort in attempting to be this person. Even though I ended each day feeling I had failed, that I hadn't been any version of enough, at least I'd been trying. At least I could try again tomorrow. The life I always wanted was forever before me, tantalisingly close — if only I could get my shit together.

These ideals had blinded me, hoodwinked me; stopped me from seeing the truth. But here I was, at the end of myself. I realised that the desire to keep improving myself to reach an impossible standard had cost me my emotional, mental and physical health.

It wasn't easy to let go of that life, of those standards. It left me feeling untethered.

The map I'd been using was useless. I didn't know where I was going. When I tried to figure out which way to go I was in Wonderland, with the Cheshire Cat replying, "well, that depends on where you want to get to."
I didn't know.
I was a stranger here.

To move forward was to embrace the unknown.
Who would I be if I wasn't trying to be this version of enough? Those first few weeks I felt relieved to have stepped off the treadmill of my own life, but I was also terrified.

A boat lost at sea.

I also felt exposed. Not in front of friends or family, that would come later, but to myself.
It's odd to realise you've been lying to yourself. Telling yourself you're happy and living the life you want, when in reality you're falling apart. The masks I'd worn to help me cope and make sense of my life had suddenly vanished. There was nothing left to rely on; no lie I could tell myself, no story I could write. The act I had been putting on – the one in which I had it all together and didn't need any help was revealed to be a sham; a charade. I found an emptiness where once apparent vitality had been.

Confronted with reality, I asked what was left of me when I put down my need to be strong and capable and good? I didn't recognise myself.

On that first day, I sat with my therapist and let myself fall apart, releasing my perception of control. My back had been against a door for so long, trying to hold back the pain and fear and failure. But I had collapsed from the strain, the door was open and the truth flooded me.

Depression didn't look like sadness. It looked like not knowing who I was anymore. It looked like always being afraid and always feeling overwhelmed. It looked like words swimming on the page and a heavy sense of exhaustion. It looked like the end of hope; an organ removed while I slept.

As I recognised the hollowness at the centre of my life, I knew one thing: I could never go back. I couldn't retrace my steps and return to a land of synthetic substances. A place where nothing really satisfied, but I pretended it did; where nothing really tasted good, but I smiled like it did; where I could never find true rest, even though I closed my eyes and feigned sleep.

Where I was headed?
That was what I had to learn.

K is for

Kick the Bucket

So, now what?
I was worn out and full
of something that sat between
shame and sadness.
I saw my therapist regularly.
In one of those first therapy sessions she
used an analogy I found very helpful.
She referred to me as a bucket.
(I know. Go with it.)

She explained:
When we're well and our needs are being met, our bucket
is full. We give to people out of the overflow of water. It is
good to give, we have enough. We enjoy sharing.
When a stressful situation occurs (a busy week; an increase
in responsibilities; A child is ill; exam stress; lack of sleep),
the bucket loses some of its water. It gets knocked and some
water splashes over the side. It's no longer full.
When this happens the emotionally healthy person
recognises this deficit and takes some time out. They rest, or
do what they need to do to recharge their batteries. Or
to continue with the analogy, to re-fill their bucket. And on
they go.

When I was first diagnosed, my therapist told me my bucket
was totally empty.

There was nothing in it.   It was completely dry.

It didn't matter if I slept well at night, or Matt took the kids out for the day and gave me a break. There would still only be drops in the bottom of the bucket. I was running on empty. On my own I was going to struggle to re-fill my bucket – especially given I had a 5-month-old, a 3-year-old, a 5-year-old, and a load of other responsibilities I couldn't yet see past. I'd been over-functioning. Pushing past the warning signs. Pushing past anything that would try and slow me down. I needed to put some fuel in the tank; some water in the bucket.

So, although there were lots of practical things I could do (and many more things I needed to stop doing, as it became apparent), I was going to need some help. My therapist told me she didn't think lifestyle changes were going to be enough to help me begin to get well.
This was how she first explained to me she thought it would be good if I went on a course of antidepressants.

I found this thought horrific. As someone who eschews drugs of any kind – I hardly ever take paracetamol for a headache, and hadn't been on the contraceptive pill for years (it made me hormonal and sad) – I found this difficult to come to terms with.

  In my secret heart, I'd always thought taking
  antidepressants was for the weak and lazy.

It was a quick-fix cure for people who weren't willing to put in the hard work. But I was the ill person, this was now clear. And someone I trusted, who was trained and knew what she was talking about, had recommended I get some chemical assistance.   I decided to go with her advice.

It was a Thursday when I managed to get to the doctor's without my pre-schoolers in tow. I was dreading it. In the time between seeing my therapist and the day I walked to the surgery (about one week) I'd gone from having compassion for myself, to thinking I was a failure and everyone knew it.

I made an effort to look like a woman who was holding it all together, not a terrified person on a rollercoaster of emotions. I couldn't bear the idea of being another one of the masses, queuing up for pills because they couldn't deal with normal life. I wanted to look assured, together. Or, at least, not deranged. I sat in the waiting room, as far away from the ill people as I could (because: panic attacks), tracing the pattern on the carpet with my heel. It took all my strength to stay in the chair and wait.

Then my name was called.

It didn't go well. The doctor (who I'd never seen before) listened to my garbled attempt to describe my symptoms and experiences, before telling me that she wasn't at all convinced I needed antidepressants and probably just needed a good night's sleep.

This totally threw me.

I was only just coming round to the idea of taking antidepressants and still wasn't sure Matt thought it was a good idea.

The last thing I needed was a medical professional questioning my decision. I had summoned all my courage to make the appointment, and now I was being refused the thing I didn't want but knew I needed.

I went home and cried with desperation.
Why did it have to be so hard?

I didn't have any energy left to keep fighting.

Somehow, a few days later I gathered my last scraps of resolve and went back for a second attempt. This time I was armed with more coherent information: a case in my favour. My therapist had previously asked me to fill out a basic mental health questionnaire (a GAD (Generalised Anxiety Disorder)-7 assessment). This very simple question and answer form looks at stress and anxiety levels. Mine were very high. (I scored 20 out of a possible 21).

Being able to name this test, as well as refer to the therapy I'd been undergoing, convinced my GP to prescribe me the drugs I really needed.

Writing this is challenging because a part of me still doesn't like the idea that I need medication. I'd rather be vigilant about preventing the circumstances that can lead to depression and anxiety than be held hostage to chemically-induced stability. Accepting my need for medication has been a humbling process. Another reminder that life is outside of my control. Another prompt to keep changing and being open.

I'm sure antidepressants are over-prescribed and, in certain cases, therapy and lifestyle changes are enough; they can heal you. But I'm also learning that sometimes, with all the good will and hard work in the world, medication is necessary.

And I'm continually reminding myself that this is okay.
In fact, it is more than okay.

It's good.

Dear Matt

Do you remember the day you told me of your epiphany? Standing in the kitchen by the bookcase, you said the most ludicrous thing.

You said; "I have just realised, I should never have expected you to be perfect."

We weren't rowing and you weren't being antagonistic, this was a new revelation to you. I think I might have laughed in response, but you were serious. You had just understood for the first time that you had placed me on a pedestal and expected me to be your 'perfect other half'; to understand you fully and work in beautiful symbiotic partnership with you. In a way it was hilarious because I had been so far from perfect, but you always were a romantic. You wanted to believe in the Hollywood ending even when I kept disappointing you.

On that day, when you returned from walking by the river, you said you were sorry, it was unreasonable. You now saw your expectation of perfection was not realistic or fair.

For the first time your view of me was unobstructed: you truly saw me.

My unrealistic expectations were always directed inward: about who I was and how I behaved. Yours were projected outward: about what our life would be like and how we would partner together.

We both believed our expectations were not pie in the sky but our right, a given. We both thought they should be fulfilled with little or no work, that parenthood and partnership, building a fulfilling life together, should come naturally.

But there was a gaping void between our expectations of how it was going to be and the reality we inhabited. And so, in the first decade of our marriage, while I was slowly being pulled under by a depression I was yet to name, space opened up between us. A space filled with disappointments we dared not speak.

I became cold. I couldn't tell you when it started. Probably in those baby years when I saw you leaving every morning for work to your important job where, among the stress and responsibility, you were admired and respected. And you got a lunch hour. Meanwhile I was plodding through the day. Occasionally finding moments of joy hidden in the drudgery. Often lonely and bored. When you returned home tired out after a day of stimulating work with clients and colleagues I was resentful.

It was unfair of me. I knew this was how we had decided to divide the responsibilities for now. I had wanted to be a mum who stayed at home with the kids when they were little, but I felt hard done by. I was weary with the routine and the constant demands.

I believed my life was harder than yours and from that seed, bitterness grew.

My distance was self-preservation. I feared you would ask more from me and I had nothing left to give. It was easier to turn away, to remove the possibility of connection and intimacy. There were many evenings when, after we'd finally got the kids to bed, you wanted to talk, to try to bridge the gap between us. When you asked if I was okay, instead of being honest I said, "No, really, I'm fine. I'm just really tired." I didn't look you in the eye in case you glimpsed the lie. I turned the television on. The space between us grew.

A competitive exhaustion had infected me. You became my adversary. I was always in a battle with you, fighting to have some time off, a break, a rest.

But then one day, the ground moved and a crack opened up in the facade we had been living. I think it was listening to that podcast that started it. You had suggested we listen together and although the thought of this made my skin crawl I had no good excuse and so we did. And as we listened to a couple we had never met discuss their marriage, we somehow found the bravery to begin to ask questions of our own. And to respond honestly.

It was painful and scary to talk about how I really felt, to trust you with my fractured heart knowing you didn't have the skills to put it back together.

It was a risk, but it was a start.
We had begun.

is for Listening

As I began the slow path to recovery I noticed a phrase my therapist often used:

> **"That must be really hard for you."**

She would listen to me talking about what had happened and how I felt, then respond;
"That must be really hard for you."

This wasn't sarcasm or pity, it was acknowledgement:
living was difficult.
I found this hard – or maybe strange – to hear.
Strange to hear this said with sincerity and kindness.
Strange for someone to look at my life, at all I was experiencing, and consider it hard.

Somewhere along the way, I'd picked up the idea that any expression of emotions on the negative side of the scale was unhelpful and unnecessary.

Emotions were not created equal.
Positive emotions: joy, gratitude and hope were to be applauded; while their more negative counterparts: sorrow, fear and shame, needed hiding. These emotions should be neither seen nor heard.

When I encountered a stressful situation, I believed my ability to see the positive side revealed a strong, holy heart. Allowing negative emotions to slip out revealed a lack of backbone. People who coped with more and maintained an upbeat attitude were worth more. I'd been told the story of the Israelites in the desert – how they had moaned and complained and, because of this, lost their way, not reaching the promised land for 40 years. I thought that if I complained I'd end up lost or forgotten. I wouldn't reach my promised land of plenty: of peace and no more anxiety.

I lived in the West and knew Jesus, surely there must be an explanation for my pain? A way of reframing it to put a positive spin on it? There had to be a lesson to learn; an alternative outcome I hadn't envisioned.

When disappointment threatened to escape like a sob
caught in my throat, I swallowed hard and sought the
purpose in it all. I fought to find a reason for my pain and
not complain about how it hurt. Because it did.
The pain was painful.

I tried to starve these emotions of oxygen.
To pretend they didn't exist.
I think you might call it denial.

As I met with my therapist I could no longer avoid the
state I was in. As I talked and lowered my guard her words
allowed me to be honest about how I felt. When she
regularly repeated, "that must be really hard for you," it was
like a long drink of water on a very hot day.

Refreshing. Offering relief.

Her words told me that what I was experiencing was real, it
was legitimate. My feelings were valid.

This was hard.
It did hurt.
I was exhausted and disappointed and felt worthless and
hopeless.
I was scared all the time and didn't know how to rest.

That must be really hard for you.
Acknowledgement.
I breathed a little easier.
I wasn't used to this kind of gracious honesty.

M

is for

Motherhood

There's a yellow rose in my garden being slowly strangled by bindweed. The vine has climbed the stem and wrapped itself around the buds. It's hard to tell where the rose ends and the weed begins.

My experience of motherhood and my experience of mental illness are similarly entwined. Being a mother has affected my mental health and my mental health has affected my experience of being a mother. It's hard to separate one from the other.

To begin at the beginning is to start with expectations. My expectations.

Poor diary management and unreliable contraceptive methods found me pregnant at 23. This unplanned pregnancy took some getting used to. Accepting it meant abandoning, or at least delaying, other plans. Six weeks of raging hormones, and emotions that swung from frustration to eventual joy passed, and I reached the appointment for my 12-week scan.

Here I was told without ceremony or emotion that no heartbeat could be found. (The doctor on duty that day needed to improve her bedside manner).
The baby had died.

I cried for days as my body emptied itself. Purging dreams and possibilities. Dumbstruck and feeling like a failure, I was angry with my body for not doing what I thought should come naturally. What was the point? I hadn't even wanted to have a baby, and – when I'd finally turned my mind in the direction my body was already walking – I had slammed into a dead end.
It was unfair. I was in shock.

As the weeks passed I became sure my grief must have a purpose. I had no way to understand or accept suffering which arrived without a life lesson to teach me.
This must be preparation for something else, a necessary step on the road. How else could I make sense of it?

One year later I'm back in the hospital. This time my pregnancy planned and much longed for. Everything goes smoothly and I give birth to Amy.

I am a Mother.
I wrap Amy up, cradle her in my arms and look into her big blue eyes. Six pounds thirteen ounces of perfection.
My heart swells and bursts.

I have a lot to learn but I feel ready.
Determined it is going to be good.

After what I'd been through, surely joy was the only possible outcome? I held her close and whispered promises to her about the kind of mother I'd be.

Relaxed, spontaneous, creative, and attentive.

Blending my mother's ease with people – and her ability to cater for crowds at the drop of a hat – with my creative temperament. I envisioned a home of happy chaos. A childhood as depicted in Shirley Hughes illustrations. Children in home-made fancy dress exploring imaginary worlds. Wild flowers and muddy knees. Dens under tables and paint-splattered faces.

This was not how it was.

That first summer, in a sleep-deprived haze caring for a baby who liked to cry, reality set in.

It was gruelling in a way I hadn't anticipated. I became increasingly desperate for structure, a plan, a way through the haze of nappies and feeds and pacing the floor with her in my arms. Something that would show me how to survive this. I longed for sleep, for personal space.

I needed a routine.

Through bloody-minded perseverance, with Gina Ford as my guide, I carved one out.

I squeezed our lives into a strict schedule, sacrificing spontaneity for predictability. It felt necessary. A short nap mid-morning, a long nap at lunch, and bedtime always at the same time. This routine became my sanity. I clawed back my evenings and an hour or two to catch up on chores in the day. It was good, this slight feeling of control.

But the relief was short-lived. The more I practised this routine, the more attached to it I became. I was fearful any interruption would cause my day to collapse.

If I could have recognised my post-natal depression at the time I would have told you it didn't feel like a lack of love or attachment to my child. I loved Amy deeply. She was perfect, healthy, beautiful.

The summer she was born Natasha Bedingfield topped the charts and I sang to Amy over and over again, *'These words are my own, from my heart flow: I love you, I love you, I love you, I love you'.*

My problem was not with her, it was with me. I wasn't good enough at motherhood. There was no ease in my days. Depression made life feel dangerous. I was holding my breath and walking on tiptoe. Caring for my child well was a precarious thing, something I could easily get wrong. Staying in control through any means necessary became imperative and, any time the day didn't work out how I had planned – when Amy missed a nap, fussed over a feed or woke too early – I felt scared, vulnerable.

A failure.

This wasn't how I thought it would feel. The fulfilment I anticipated in the acts of playing and providing a safe and warm home weren't forthcoming. I wondered what I was doing wrong. How could I find the job satisfaction I craved? How could I dial down the anxiety that was creeping in? I was working as hard as I could. But the signs to let me know if I was doing an okay job weren't easy to read. I wanted a performance review. Someone to talk me through my strengths and weaknesses and what was best practice. To improve my game and applaud my efforts.

Over the next six years we added two more babies to our brood and then, only then, was I diagnosed with post-natal depression.

Despite adoring my children, life had become black and white. My friend said I looked like I had been filtered: a photograph with the warmth and colour removed. Which was how I felt.

This certainly wasn't the free-wheeling care-free time I'd hoped for.

Over the years, I've given some thought to my initial diagnosis of post-natal depression and wondered whether this was accurate.

> Was my depression triggered in some way by becoming a mother?

The pressure and hormonal changes, the loss of any sense of self, sacrificed for their needs?

> Honestly, I don't know.

I do know however that motherhood magnified the symptoms of my depression and the disruption of my sleep exacerbated any underlying mental illness. The relentlessness of motherhood created a crucible for my anxiety, making it glow with a white heat I couldn't escape.

It's hard to write about what I got wrong and all the ways I would have done it differently, had I known. But I can't live with regret, wishing I had behaved or felt differently in those years when my girls were squishy-thighed toddlers. I am learning to recognise the me I was back then was doing her best. And I am learning to love her.

She drove herself into the ground, eventually making herself ill; but she loved her children. And, as I forgive myself, I'm recovering memories of good days: picnics at National Trust houses, dancing in the kitchen, paddling at the beach, reading and re-reading favourite books, snuggling on the sofa.

I didn't get everything right, but I was loving my kids in the best way I knew how.

N IS FOR NO

Post-diagnosis, although it was clear there was a lot that had to change, there were many things I still had to do: non-negotiable responsibilities.

I took the girls to school and spent the days caring for my energetic toddler. I made the tea and helped with homework. I put the kids to bed and kept on top of the laundry, mostly.

Everything else I had known was slowly coming apart in my hands, but these practical tasks kept me moving through the days. This routine made me feel safe, it gave me a structure when everything else felt uncertain and scary.

Apart from these basic requirements, much had to change. I had to learn how to think in a different way, letting go of the idea that my worth was attached to my ability to do it all.

I started small.

Baby steps towards creating the space I needed.

With no fanfare, I slipped out of weekly commitments that were previously set in stone. I didn't have the stomach to be upfront about this, so for a while I fudged it. I made excuses. I said I was ill, or one of the kids were. I said I couldn't get a babysitter.

I became inconsistent and unreliable.

I wasn't ready to make big decisions about how I wanted to use my time, or have hard conversations about how I was going to be letting others down. I would have to build toward this level of honesty. Week-by-week, I gave myself permission to ignore texts and phone calls, and to side-step events I knew I'd find draining or too tiring.

At home, I trained myself to become less bothered about the things that didn't matter. The house was messier and the kids went for longer without baths. We ate beige food from the freezer more regularly and watched more television. Home slowly became a sanctuary where I could hide and begin to recover. I hunkered down and kept the real world out as much as possible.

> As the months passed, the list of activities I stepped out of grew.

I built the muscle of volition, gaining confidence to make decisions about my life in my own best interests.

Before my crash-out, I was someone who was good at volunteering and leading, making suggestions and organising events. I was the person who would bring a home-made cake or throw a surprise party, and often both at the same time. I was the first to offer to host, or provide the food, or organise the joint present. I was the one to make plans and coordinate dates. I slowly began to pry open my fingers and release the responsibilities that had kept me moving so fast I was permanently exhausted.

> I'd always believed a busy person was a good person. I'd looked to my busyness to gauge how important or popular I was. If I was in demand, I knew I mattered.

I had to re-think those ideas. If I had free time and space, did that mean I was worth less than someone who filled every minute of their week? Did it make me lazy or irrelevant? The lie that my worth was attached to my activity clung to me and raised its head often. The idea was sticky. Hard to shake off.

But I knew it was essential to create space for recovery. Quietening and slowing down my life was the only way out of the haze of anxiety and back to health. Treating myself with this level of kindness was a challenge. I had to regularly remind myself why I was making these changes and how necessary they were. To live without busyness as a status symbol was new. It left me feeling untethered, not knowing how to measure my life.

I cancelled plans.

In the moment, I might feel I was missing out by not attending, but often the cost of going was too high. Anything that depleted my energy reserves – anything that wasn't nourishing to me – had to go. Naming things helped. I replaced my Fear Of Missing Out (FOMO) with a new concept. Joy of Missing Out (JOMO) turned staying home from feeling like a failure, to feeling like a treat. I was not staying home because I couldn't cope. I was staying home because I wanted to look after myself. JOMO often involved pyjamas, nice food and a quiet relaxing space.
I was learning how to treat myself.

It wasn't easy. Early on, my therapist taught me it can be necessary to say 'no' a number of times before people will accept your answer and stop asking. When you've always behaved in a certain way, people reasonably rely on you and expect you to respond as you previously have done.
I didn't even look ill. In public, I mostly managed to pull

myself together to appear as though I was coping. I wore clean clothes and brushed my hair. My kids were as well turned out as they ever had been. There were no warnings or signs to alert friends and colleagues I'd changed. Unless I chose to bare my soul about the state of my mental health, there was no reason anyone would know why I refused to volunteer, why I didn't show up where I previously would have. I didn't make an announcement or send a group email to let everyone know I was slowing down. I had to accept the inevitable disappointment people felt in me.

I also quietly distanced myself from a few friends who'd been leaning heavily on me for emotional support. This might have been the hardest thing. Two friends I loved dearly were going through storms of their own. Serious pain and grief. I felt I was abandoning them. It hurt my heart to let them down, to not be the person they could turn to. I had to regularly remind myself that my health had to come first. I was on the floor; I couldn't carry them.

I know they felt my absence as a kind of betrayal. But it was the only thing I could do. My therapist was very clear with me. I would only get well if I put myself first, above friends and family, above everyone else's needs and expectations.

As a card carrying people-pleaser, this pained me greatly. Every time self-doubt came knocking, telling me that my friends were sick of my absence and lack of engagement – that I was letting people down and would soon be forgotten about – I reminded myself that this was how it had to be. I cried at how weak and impotent I felt and steeled myself against their confusion and frustration.

This was the only way to get well.

IS FOR OUGHT, SHOULD AND MUST

As I started to say 'no', I realised my self-worth wasn't only tied to what I did. I had also tied it to who I believed I should be.

It wasn't just about the activities I performed. It was about who I was: the essential essence of me.
My identity.
My sense of self.

Who was I, when I wasn't busy doing good things?

What was left?

The ideas in my mind about what made a good person were etched indelibly.

Ought, should and must weren't just external expectations but, like a stick of rock, they were written through my core. Wife, mother, obedient daughter, ambitious creative, gracious hostess, available friend. I needed rousing from my stupor. I needed to question the roles I played, that added up to who I thought I should be.

Situated in Liverpool's Georgian Quarter, the Italian restaurant was busy and familiar. I sat on a bench, my back to the wall, Matt and Mark opposite me. Mark had been working as Matt's business mentor for a number of years. At home, Matt spoke so often about the perspective and wisdom Mark had brought to his work I'd taken to rolling my eyes at the mention of his name.

Eventually, I succumbed to Matt's requests and agreed to have dinner with them. A relaxed meal for me to get to know the man who'd become an important friend to my husband.

The evening wasn't what I expected. Our conversation surprised me.

We sat down and Mark began asking questions about my life and how it was changing. Matt had obviously talked about me to Mark – about the journey I was on and how I was re-learning how to live. Mark listened attentively and reflected back to me what I was saying, clarifying the realisations I was coming to; the new possibilities I was beginning to see about how my life could be.

I liked the version of me he called out; the me he saw. And I liked that my husband heard me described in this way.

It was as though his confidence in my ability to change my life gave me the courage to talk freely for the first time.

As we talked together and Mark made observations, I began to re-imagine myself. I'd felt so disappointed, so ashamed and tired but now, over pasta and red wine, I began to see things could be different. For the first time in a long time I started to think about what I wanted.

Honestly, the whole experience was a little odd. I felt emotionally undone, vulnerable. I kept looking to Matt for any sign he was uncomfortable about the nature of our conversation, but he just smiled at me, occasionally interjecting to clarify something I was saying, or to make a bad joke.
I wondered for a moment if I'd been set up, if Matt had engineered this whole meeting.

We finished our main course and it was then that Mark said something which left me stunned.
He told me I needed to think about whether I wanted to be married or stay and raise my children.
He said I could leave my husband and my children if that would be better for me, for my health, for my life. It was a real option.
I could do something new – something different with my life.
I could start again and pursue whatever other dreams I had.
He told me I was allowed to choose.

He wasn't giving me permission, it wasn't his to give. He was showing me I had the permission already. My life was in my hands.

Mark told me to take at least the weekend before I made my decision.

Something in the pit of my stomach told me not to brush past this. It was important.

I knew I couldn't ignore or make a joke of it.
This was a sacred moment.

I went outside to get some fresh air. I needed to be away
from the table for a moment. To be alone. Who was this
man and what was he saying? And why was my husband
sat next to him so calmly? I laughed out loud.
What was happening?

I pulled my jacket around me in the cool of the evening,
watching the cars pass. I looked at the sky. For a moment, it
felt as if the hard crust of disappointment and resignation
– everything about what I believed my life had to be, the
duty and responsibility – was breaking off me. As though I
was breathing fresh air for the first time in years.

Mark was pushing me to decide what I wanted from life.
He was provoking me to think about the kind of life I
would choose, and to choose it. I had always been good and
accepted the expectations that came with that. The oughts
and shoulds and musts were part of an ingrained mindset,
where I abdicated responsibility for my life and let this set
of standards tell me who to be.

I had to question everything. Even the parts of my life I had
thought inviolable.
Should I stay married?
Should I raise my children?

I needed to take control of my own life and stop being
bullied by what I thought was expected of me.

This kind of thinking was beyond me.
It felt extraordinary.
As I stood in the cold I felt a smile creep over my face. And a
weight fall from my shoulders. I stood a little taller.

I was allowed to make these kinds of decisions.
It was up to me.
It was my life.

I'd never learnt to make decisions for myself. I hadn't ever
really rebelled or gone off the rails.
Being good had kept me safe, but it hadn't given me the
skills to shape a life of my own.
I had been treading in someone else's footprints, unable to
deviate from the path set out before me. I needed to change.
I needed to choose my life.

And so, to take him at his word, I took the weekend.
I thought about it. I gave my marriage and my children
serious consideration.

Did I want this life?

Was it going to enable me to be most fully me?

> I did.
> I chose them.
> I chose to be married to my husband; I loved him.
> I chose to care for my children; to love them and
> to raise them.
> I chose my life.

And I continue to learn to choose.
To rid my life of oughts and shoulds and musts.

I'm a grown up and I get to choose. I must not forget it.

P is for Practical and Physical

My diagnosis and the changes in the way I thought about what made a worthwhile life were going to take time to get to grips with. There was no short-cut. Meanwhile I was still mentally, emotionally and physically exhausted. I needed to regroup. I needed time for the antidepressants to kick in, which they did, slowly.

Over the months following my diagnosis, energy was gradually restored. Little by little, day by day. I learnt to take an active role in my recovery as the chemical support stabilised me. I gained understanding, learnt new skills and developed new habits. I undertook the long-term process of re-evaluating my mindsets and relationships. And, at the same time, became proactive about the practical and physical changes I could make to fight the most brutal aspects of my mental illness: anxiety and panic.

Sometimes it was too hard to think about all the big ideas about who I was and who I could be; the internal, messy stuff. Some days, most days, I just needed to get through. Having practical ways to increase my level of calm was helpful.

1 Reduce my caffeine intake.

I realised there was a direct correlation between how much caffeine I consumed and how on edge I felt. Not surprising, I know. Reducing my intake increased my ability to know calm. I replaced coffee with tea, or tea with peppermint tea, or sometimes hot water (how virtuous I felt on those days!). When I was having a particularly anxious few days, or felt stress creeping in, I would cut down and only have one to two cups of tea a day. (I could easily drink five otherwise).

2 Go outside.

Even when exercise felt impossible I would try and go outside, if only for a few moments. Even standing on my front step and breathing in the fresh air and feeling the sun or rain on my face, benefitted me. If I could, I went for a short walk – even just around the block. This decision not only sent a sign to my brain that I was willing to prioritise what I needed, but being outdoors also had a grounding, stabilising effect on me. It still does. As I move in the fresh air, acknowledging my inability to control the weather and recognising the physical sensation of my body connecting to the earth, I feel grounded and gain fresh perspective.

3 Cancel something.

A life-changing revelation: I discovered my diary does not own me. As I learnt to think about my capacity, I stopped listening to the voice of obligation telling me I shouldn't cancel a meeting or activity. Instead, I started to pay attention to the voice inside that was telling me to give myself a break and offer myself grace. It helped to imagine the person I was cancelling on was probably also very busy and might welcome this cancellation or postponement. The world wouldn't end if I went slower.

4 Write it down.

Sometimes my brain was such a jumble I had no idea how I ended up feeling so overwhelmed and overcommitted. I had so many tabs open I'd find myself reacting, not responding. Writing out how I felt and what was going through my mind became an excellent way of keeping track. It enabled me to make sense of thought patterns that were confusing and gave me the opportunity to take back control of the messages I was listening to. It also helped me to reflect and see patterns in my behaviour and thoughts – to look back to enable me to look forward and make plans.

5 Treat myself.

Being kind to myself was not something that came naturally. I was used to being far more attentive to everyone else, their needs and concerns. I gradually learnt that I had needs and concerns too, and I could attend to them. It didn't have to be something huge. Sometimes it looked like sitting down and drinking my cup of tea while it was still hot or walking around my garden in the evening noticing the flowers that had bloomed that day. I tried to factor in some self care every week. When I started this practice it felt self-indulgent, naughty even. But it was essential. Weekly, or even daily practice reminded me I deserved to be looked after too; that I was a person of worth. For caregivers this isn't something we remember easily. But I began to see it was essential to love me first.

6 Seek beauty.

I'd been so busy I'd stopped seeing and looking for beauty. Slowing down, I made a conscious effort to look for beauty in unexpected places, or at unexpected times. I embraced whimsy, picking up leaves on the school run, arranging my food thoughtfully on my plate, tracing the patterns in the rain on the window, stopping to take photos of the light and the shadows, the latest flower that bloomed, the blossom on the tree. Being in the moment had a calming effect and brought great joy to me. Recognising everyday beauty is a holy act.

7   Limit screen time.

When I was diagnosed, although I already had a phone
I took everywhere, it hadn't yet become a compulsion
to check social media all the time. As the world of
Instagram and Facebook has encroached further and new
opportunities to connect appear daily, I find it necessary to
have rules about how I use my phone. I leave it downstairs
at night to charge and try and have an hour before it's
turned on in the morning.

If I recognise I've been spending too much time scrolling
aimlessly – comparing other peoples' curated lives with
my reality – I try and have a break; to leave my phone at
home when I go out or turn it off earlier in the evening. I
don't always manage this, but when I do it's good. There
are countless studies that prove the connection between
too much screen time and increased levels of anxiety. It's
become vital for me to think about how I engage online and
how much time I spend in front of a screen.

∫ Tell someone.

When I was struggling or I could feel a panic attack rising within me, if I was able to, I made a friend aware of what was going on. Rather than struggling on alone, allowing my thoughts to play havoc chasing me around in circles, I learnt to reach out and connect with someone else. This brought me back to the earth, reminded me I wasn't a failure (which is a tune that would play on a loop when I was spiralling) and developed trust in some key friendships. My friend Laura suggested we had a code word, that could be sent up like the illuminated sign over Gotham city (or Liverpool) to let her know when I was struggling.

Our Bat-Signal was a text message which literally contained the words "Bat-Signal" (inventive, no?). This wasn't her call to jump into action and fly over to me, but she might send me an encouraging text reminding me of some truth I knew already but had temporarily forgotten, or a simple graphic I could use to slow my breathing down. Sometimes she would do nothing, but the simple fact I'd taken action stopped me feeling powerless and isolated.

Q is for Quiet

My brain was a jumble. It was used to activity and managing stress; to being on high alert for any potential harm headed my way. It was a noisy place to live. I needed quiet, but this wasn't easy. I couldn't simply tell my mind to quieten and have it obey. I needed to learn how.

At the time, I didn't understand mindfulness and thought meditation was some Paul McKenna manipulative nonsense.

I hadn't considered the possibility that these practices could be helpful, that they would change me. The idea of making time to sit and do nothing still fitted too neatly into the category of time wasting and self-indulgence. I had no desire to sit chanting or to make a shrine.
Thankfully, the skills I learnt demanded neither.
(Also, I'm sure chanting and shrine building are incredibly helpful to some, they just aren't my bag.)

Learning these practices allowed me to become attuned to what was going on in my body and mind. It enabled me to recognise the warning signs when panic was rising.

Meditation re-educated me about what a new 'normal' could feel like.

> I learnt:
> If we weren't neurotic crazies, encumbered by stress and busyness, we would take between six and eight breaths a minute. If we breathed like this we would be filling our lungs in the best way possible, expelling all carbon dioxide. Our bodies would be operating how they should and we'd be far more relaxed. Our stress levels would be lower and we'd feel the physical benefits throughout our bodies.

But, we don't.

Our full and frantic lives ensure we breathe like we do everything else: too fast.
I had to start with the very basic building blocks. I had to learn how to breathe again.
My therapist began by teaching me seven-eleven breathing. The concept is remarkably straight forward. You breathe in for seven counts and out for eleven counts. The numbers aren't important – only that the exhale is longer than the inhale.

She then added to this practice of stillness and quiet by introducing a number of different techniques over the weeks.

Firstly, body scanning.

With my eyes closed, she asked me to draw attention to one part of my body, then another. I was to tense and then relax that group of muscles to ensure I wasn't holding any excess tension anywhere. I was to breathe into this area of the body, focusing my mind on the sensations and relaxing it as

I was able. Through this process I was amazed at how and where my body was storing stress (my jaw, always my jaw). The simple act of recognising this and choosing to relax and release the tension brought increased levels of calm. I started to experience a peace I hadn't known for many years.

Next, my therapist talked me through relaxation with visualisation.

As I sat on my sofa, again with my eyes shut, she would talk to me about a beautiful place. For me this was often a beach. She would paint a picture of the scene, the walk through the sand dunes, the sounds of the waves, the feeling of sun on my skin. She would invite me to relax here, to lie on the sand feeling its warmth on my back, my senses alive to the beauty and complete rest of the moment.

It was hard to stop my mind racing away in these guided meditations. I started wondering if there was a toilet or clean water available on the beach. (Yes, I needed to know there were facilities nearby, even in my imagination). I struggled to focus on the picture being drawn for me. Regularly, my therapist would remind me to bring the attention back to the breath or the visualisation. She encouraged me not to chastise myself for losing concentration, but to be aware of it and gently bring my attention back.

A small part of me – the smart arse, the critic – sat outside of me, looking on, telling me I was ridiculous and this was a waste of my time. It couldn't possibly make any difference. Another part of me felt anxious, even while meditating. I'd been holding everything so tightly for such a long time, that to relax muscles and give my mind and attention over to my therapist felt scary.

A part of me was sure that as soon as I stopping being hyper-vigilant and relaxed my guard, something bad would happen. I don't know what I thought this might be. But I'd been so controlled and vigilant about what I saw and heard and came into contact with, the idea of lowering my defences was terrifying.

Thankfully, a larger part of me was engaged with the meditation. I silenced the critic who told me it was nonsense and wouldn't work, and the fear that told me it would make me worse. I learnt to enter in. My breathing began to slow and my muscles relaxed. I started to see the benefit of these sessions.

My therapist encouraged me to practise these techniques at home, making sure I painted a picture for the visualisation with as much detail as possible, including all the senses. What could I see; feel; hear; smell and taste? The richer the picture, the greater chance I would enter in.

Meditation taught my brain how to relax, and gave me tools with which to fight anxiety when it tried to barge its way in. Through repeated practice (and I wasn't a good student – my learning was far from consistent) I improved my skills and my brain started to remember these new healthier ways to be. I started to change my mind.

Now I knew there was an alternative.
A way out.

It may not yet have been a well-worn route from panic to calm, but I was starting to form new neural pathways. The more I walked on this path, the more well-defined and easy to navigate it became.

R is for Relapse

My recovery hasn't been a straight line from bottom left to top right of the page: a graph of growing health with no deviations.

I wish it had.

After 18 months on my initial prescription of antidepressants, I felt well enough to start lowering my dosage. I discussed this with my therapist and doctor and was careful not to go cold turkey. I took half doses, then half doses every other day, before stopping completely.

And it was good.

Over the next few years I took jobs at the theatre. I loved being back in the rehearsal room – the buzz of a company figuring out a new show, the intensity of tech week, the production opening to the public. My self-esteem swelled. I made tentative approaches to re-engage with church, attending again and gradually feeling part of the family.

But life was not perfect. My husband left a business he'd grown from the ground up and managed for 15 years. This was painful and unsettling. There were complications in our wider family, relationships weren't plain sailing and we experienced unexpected bereavements. It wasn't easy, but I was well enough to be able to listen, support Matt and give him some processing space, as he did for me.

Then in 2015, gradually, so I didn't recognise what was happening at first, I started to experience occasional blips; moments of anxiety.

These became more frequent and in the summer of 2015 I experienced a few mega Panic Attacks (necessary capitalisation).

They are forever seared onto the hard drive of my brain.

The first occurred at a restaurant with one of my oldest friends. Her second child was due imminently and I wanted to take her out for one last hurrah before the baby arrived. I planned the evening; chose the time and location to ensure a successful evening. I wasn't especially anxious. I'd been feeling calm that week and looking forward to being out of the house while my husband was battling bath and bedtime with our three kids.

It began just before she arrived. I felt twitchy, jittery.

I sought to distract myself by watching a lame comedy on TV.
Anything to silence the inner dialogue of potential disaster.

She arrived. I asked if we could stop for cigarettes on the
way. As an occasional smoker, I knew it sometimes had
a calming effect on me, snapping me out of my anxiety,
grounding me. I smoked two cigarettes quickly. We went
into the restaurant.
I was floating out of my body, observing myself.
Powerless to stop what was unfolding.

I tried to remain calm.
To make my hands lie still, to tether myself to the table.
I took deep breaths.
I asked questions, and feigned interest in the answers I was
barely hearing.
I fought to conceal the sweating, circling, churning.
The awareness of my body's internal workings.

Every stimulus, every synapse, every nerve ending was on
high alert.

I went to the bathroom and splashed water on myself to
try and pull myself out of it. I looked in the mirror. I slapped
my own face.

I was angry and scared. Nothing was working.
I was spiralling down, unable to find a solid place to plant
my feet and get a grip. To stop me being washed away.

The food arrived. I pushed it around on my plate trying to
smile and make eye contact.

Forcing myself to try and act, to be normal.
Why couldn't I just be bloody normal?

I was wretched.
Sick. Alone.
Hot, dislocated.

Buzzing in my brain and paralysis in my body.

Fear like a wave washed over me.
Then something snapped.

"I have to go," I said. *"Now."*

She didn't argue. I paid and we left, the food almost
untouched on our plates. Then she drove me home, all the
while reassuring me that it didn't matter; that she was fine;
that she was glad I'd told her how I was feeling.
(Find a friend like mine. Friends who get it are gold.)

I opened the front door and fell into my husband's arms
sobbing, shaking, unable to speak.
The terror is unexplainable.

Later, sat on the sofa under an old blanket, my breathing
almost back to normal, I tried to process the disaster the
evening had been.
What was wrong with me? I'd been in therapy for years
now and I had been doing okay. Where did this come from?
A bolt out of the blue, an interruption to the narrative that I
was well and able to cope.

I was deeply ashamed.
And frightened.

As the weeks passed, I tried to bury my growing anxiety. I told myself it was a one-off. That this panic attack was not indicative of a deeper issue.

But this wasn't true no matter how much I repeated it. Before long I was back battling anxiety every day. The 'fight or flight' mega-dose of adrenalin had been activated and never abated. Hyper-vigilance and the heart-racing, hand-shaking that went with it became the norm. Catastrophe, my ear worm.

Even good days were tiring. The mental strength to remind myself of the truth, the vigilance needed to stay strong, to keep my feet from slipping, took every drop of willpower. I would find myself standing at the edge of the pool, focusing on my breathing, trying to take it easy. The energy used to stay on the bank, safe and dry, was great. It was exhausting. And the days when I did fall... they were awful.

I was doing my best. I was fighting, doing the things I knew to do. Eating healthily and exercising regularly. I cut back on caffeine and alcohol. I meditated most days to try create some quiet in my 100mph brain. Nothing was working.

Christmas came and went in a rush of highs and lows. I survived.

Just.

At the end of the holidays, I made an appointment to see my therapist. I unburdened myself, confiding in her about the pool, how it was always there. About how much energy it took not to fall in, about how tired I was.

Without thinking, I said,
"I wish there was a pill I could take to make it all go away."

And she looked at me. And I looked at her.

And I cried.
I cried because I felt like failure for not managing to fix myself. I cried with frustration.
And I cried with relief.

I'd been holding myself together for so long. Hope had been ebbing away. I'd started to believe that this was my lot, this was how it would always be.

I'd forgotten how it felt to live a day without anxiety.

is for

Second Time

Around

One week after seeing my therapist, one week of fighting the fear and the doubt, I saw my doctor. I told him what I'd told her. He listened, asked questions, warned me of potential side-effects and wrote me a prescription.
I walked out into the fresh air holding a potential new start written in medical words I wasn't familiar with. I cried and, as I did, two words popped into my head.

This was difficult and this was brave.

Putting down my need to fix myself, and putting aside my insecurity about what it would mean if I became someone who took antidepressants again, was hard. It was not the soft-option, the cop out, the easy thing to do. It was difficult.

And it was brave. Brave to admit I wasn't coping, to confess my weakness and my fear. Brave to hope that these pills wouldn't make my situation worse, and I would cope if there were any side-effects. Brave to believe this didn't count me out, or disqualify me. And brave to hope for something else, to believe change was possible.

> The first few weeks taking these antidepressants I was a mess.

As physical illness has always been the focus of my anxiety, taking anything new and unknown into my body was terrifying. The mess of feelings and thoughts, the many potential outcomes, the not-knowing and the imagining were a lot to deal with. My friend Laura suggested I write it all down. Before I went to bed, and sometimes during the day too, I would dump the toxicity, the spiralling thoughts, the negativity and the panic, out of my brain and into my notebook.

What follows is some of those scribblings.

Day 5: **Monday**

Brain skitting about all over the place. Anxious stomach. Can't wait for the drugs to kick in, and terrified that they won't. Last week was a better week... but yesterday and today the hyper-vigilance is back, or at least encroaching again.

The list of things I can't read or watch is growing:
— anything to do with illness (obviously)
— anything to do with children (because... just in case)
— anything connected to food (including new or unfamiliar cookery books. A new low)
—anything connected to travel (inability to control environment/ fear of the future).

Again I am wary to make plans, trying to keep my week quiet. Amanda (my therapist) and Laura (a friend) tell me to be kind to myself but I feel this is always my mantra: '...do less, say no, manage your boundaries'.
Most of me is waiting to get well so I can do more, achieve more, see more. But maybe that is all wrong. Maybe I should accept that I can't do and may never be able to what I used to do.

But that feels horribly like settling.

Looking back now, this was a fairly normal day.
Like it had been for the best part of a year.

Day 6: **Tuesday**

Really tough day. Emotional and psychological roller coaster.
Finding it very hard not to give feelings of failure room to grow.

Not trusting yourself to make lunch plans, or even coffee
plans, in case you can't cope makes it hard not to feel like a
loon. By 7pm I felt sick and shaky. So low.
There is no warning, suddenly my energy is completely
depleted, empty, nothing left.

Day 7: **Wednesday**

Awful, awful night.
Awake between 2:30-5am panicking, catastrophising and
generally despairing. Woke sweaty, anxious, exhausted. Feel
like I am losing the plot entirely. Totally envious of anyone
who wakes up feeling calm. Feel I am letting the kids down.
I am a mess. Confused. Feeling sick. Head aching. At the end
of my tether. Weak and stupid.

Later: A truly awful morning. In tears, despairing, freaking
out. As bad as it has ever been. Head aching, sick feeling.
Exhaustion. Barely held it together to pick up kids from
school. Wonder if I should be allowed to look after them at all.

Day 8: Thursday

A slightly better day. Am definitely ill with some flu-bug thing. Ed off school today so I had an enforced quiet day of crochet and the radio. Barely moved. I need more days like this.

Great chat on the phone with Sri.
Afterwards she texted me 'your war is my war'.
I am impatient. Sri encouraged me to stop before I start, ie. take some time to properly recover. I am hesitant to do this because 1. what if I still don't get better? and 2. what have the last six years been about? I feel as though I'm always saying – soon, soon I'll make that piece of work, I'll be well enough to do that job… I have these pure creative moments when I can see the work ahead of me – but then I am unable to get on with it – fear/ lack of energy/ life gets in the way and the work is continually delayed, then forgotten about.

Oh to wake tomorrow with a clear mind, no headache, no anxiety! That would be joy on joy!

Day 9: Friday

Better day, although headaches and back/ arm ache and general tiredness. Have needed lots of reassurance I won't always be like this…

$Day\ 10$: Saturday

Woke anxious but for first time in a long time I was able to make a decision to move past it. This took a huge amount of effort and focus, but I was rewarded with a good day. A day where catastrophising thoughts were few, a day where I was flexible and able to go with the flow, a day of disastrously sandy and windy walks abandoned quickly, squealing children, poor nutrition, and a hectic house with Monopoly Junior, dressing-up and cake decorating happening simultaneously.

And. I. Was. Fine.
Those four words look like hope to me.

T is for Truth

The first few weeks were rough. There's no denying it. My six-year-old crawled into bed with me one morning and asked,

"Mum, why do good days go so quick and bad days take ages?"

I wish I knew.

Looking back now, I'm surprised to find, peppered through my barely legible scrawls, words of hope and support. Words from people who loved me and were with me through it all. Even though at times I felt lonely, I was never alone.

There were also moments of clarity.

In amongst the brain fog, extreme tiredness and overwhelm, were pinpricks of light. At the point of most despair, of most acute anxiety, I have written in my notebook:

> ... As I identify another element of my brokenness,
> I shine like the morning.

When I discovered this phrase amongst the desperation, I was surprised. My emotions were screaming a different story, but this is the truth of what was happening and, on some level – even from within the confusion – I knew it. I understand this a little more every day.

Spiritual writer, Richard Rohr, puts it brilliantly:
"The path of descent is the path of transformation. Darkness, failure, relapse, death and woundedness are our primary teachers rather than ideas or doctrines."

Digging in the depths, acknowledging my suffering and being willing to sit with the pain long enough, is the path to healing, acceptance and grace.

In fact, it is the only way.

T is also for A Story About Teeth

I'm ten years old. I'm in the car on my way to school.
From my vantage point in the back seat, I can see my face in
the rear-view mirror.

I have the self-confidence of a child who knows they are
loved and is sure life is going to be just great.

I see my face: my eyes, nose and mouth, framed and
reflected back.

I look beautiful.
My big blue eyes, my clear skin, my red lips. My brown
hair pulled back off my forehead now that stupid fringe
is growing out. My dimples, my dark brows, my long
eyelashes.

I smile at myself without opening my mouth.
I keep my lips closed over my teeth.
I don't want to spoil the picture.

The years pass and I become increasingly aware and critical of the way I look.

The gap between my front teeth becomes the symbol for everything I deem wrong with my body.

The slither of dark.
I hate it.
I want my teeth to be like everyone else's.
Straight. Closed. Perfect.

I used to plan for how I would 'get my teeth fixed', only then to be spotted in a harshly-lit shopping centre by a model scout. As if the only thing standing between me and stardom (or, at least, the Clothes Show Live) was the uniformity of my smile.

At 13, I sit in the orthodontist's chair and have my first brace fitted.
The dentist tells me the gap between my teeth is large enough to justify braces. He also warns me in no uncertain terms that he's sure my teeth will gradually move back to their original position once the brace is removed.

In his mind, my dream of straight teeth was far from a definite outcome. It was unlikely, at best. This man in his white coat, in his high-ceilinged room in a posh part of town, tries to persuade me not to follow this course of action. He assures me my teeth are fine and I don't need the gap closed. "Some people even think it's a sign of prosperity," he told me. (What did he know?) It would be painful he said, and the results wouldn't be what I wanted. The gap would not remain permanently closed. He was very clear about this.

But I knew better.   He was wrong.   He just had to be.

After six months of sore and swollen lips, food stuck in between the wires and excruciating brace tightenings, the moment came for the train-tracks to be removed.

And, oh joy, it had worked!
The teeth had been forced into position. They had been made to submit to my will.
I'd been right all along!

I sat on the bus on the way home, finding every excuse to show off my continuous white smile.

However.

Despite the retainer I wore at night for numerous years, despite my hope and disbelief, slowly my teeth moved back to their original moorings.

Gradually,   the   gap   opened   up   again.

I pushed my tongue between the front teeth, willing there to be no gap.

I'd done everything right.
I'd worn my brace at night.
I'd been diligent about dental hygiene.
But there was no mistaking it.

                                                    The gap was back.

I was disappointed, dejected.
I found it hard to accept this was the way my life was meant to go, that this was my lot, my portion.
I was going to be someone who had to endure life with gappy teeth.

It took a long time to accept my smile.
For many years I longed for a different outcome.
But that wasn't the way it turned out.

It took time to accept it is my imperfections that make me, me.

That make me beautiful.

U is for Upside Down

This is the world I now inhabit.

The world I have created and curated for myself, having discarded the one I used to live in – the one that made me ill.

In the world of Upside Down my failures have become my successes.

As I have written and talked about my anxiety and depression this reality, which for so many years I was ashamed of, has made my life bigger.
Dr Cornell West writes that in order to really live we first have to learn how to die. We must die to ourselves – to our ideas of what a successful life looks like.

Last night I woke at 3am in the midst of a panic attack.
My heart was racing, beating out of my chest.
It was awful, but I was able to slow my breath, to give my body the signals it needed to understand that I was not under attack.

It was not long before I was asleep again.

This morning I felt discombobulated. Out of sorts. I wrestled with feelings of inadequacy, of shame; of fear this will always be my reality.

Then I remembered I live in the Upside Down and I don't have to feel alone and worthless; I don't have to think my suffering excludes or disqualifies me.

I still felt sad, flat, so I did something about it. I took to Instagram and wrote a series of messages about my night, and how I felt this morning. I wrote of my determination to offer myself kindness and grace today. I reminded myself that I was not weak or less because I had experienced panic. I ended with a message of love to anyone else who was struggling today.

By the time I was through writing my little messages on social media, I was already feeling better. The act of communicating, of being honest about how I felt, and reiterating the truth I know but easily forget, changed something.

I was preaching to myself.

A friend messaged me almost immediately not only to send her love and affirm me, but to let me know she was also struggling and we could be in it together.
To undo shame first we have to speak our story, then we have to let those who love us speak love back to us.

In the Upside Down world being honest about the hard things brings comfort. It doesn't exclude, it includes us. There is no need to pretend or fake it.

Our weakness is our strength.

is for Vulnerable

As a self-confessed over-sharer, who lives with my heart on my sleeve and my foot in my mouth, I always thought I was pretty honest with those around me. But, as I removed the masks of competency and self-sufficiency I had long been wearing, I realised these moments of candour were not the full story.

I was happy to talk about when I had failed – but only in an anecdote that showed the lesson I had learnt or how it all worked out in the end. I waited until the messy and painful struggles were consigned to the past, before I shared them with others.

It looked like vulnerability, but it wasn't.

Because true vulnerability is not formed in the past tense. It can only be known in the present.

When I returned home after my third therapy session to tell my husband about my diagnosis and the prescription I now knew I needed, it was awkward. I didn't know how to have this conversation. I didn't really understand it myself and to try and explain it to someone else felt almost impossible.

I was full of fear and didn't know what the future might hold. I told Matt about the bucket and how tired I was. I told him about the drugs and how I hoped they would help.

I felt raw and exposed.
It seemed so loaded, so potentially volatile.

I wanted him to jump straight to acceptance without any processing time himself. I needed him to offer me reassurance and felt frustrated when he wasn't able to; when he had questions or said he was exhausted himself. It was hard.

We navigated those first few months. We learnt together and somehow found a way through, taking it one day at a time.

Remaining open was not easy.
Life was changing. I was changing.

Often I wanted to draw back; to not express what was happening with me while it all seemed so new and fragile. To make myself vulnerable was a choice I had to make on a regular basis: to risk saying difficult things; risk revealing feelings I thought ugly. Risk his rejection. Risk the argument that might follow. Risk starting a conversation I didn't know how to finish.

Brené Brown[2] writes that vulnerability is the first thing we look for in a potential friend, but often the last thing we are willing to reveal. We want to connect with others in an honest way, but we also want to wear a mask that makes us look good. We are afraid that, if others know the truth about us – how we really feel, our fears and the pain we carry – we will be rejected.

2. p.42 from *Daring Greatly: How the courage to be vulnerable transforms the way we live, love, parent and lead*; Brené Brown

But someone has to go first.
It might as well be you.

I learnt to go first.

I started tricky conversations when it would have felt safer to keep quiet. I talked to friends and family about my diagnosis, about the panic attacks and the anxiety and how complicated everything was.

I'd love to tell you everyone welcomed the new me with open arms, but that's not true. Although many did, there were some who didn't want to hear the truth I was talking. They wanted to stay engaged with the upbeat, always-saying-yes Elli. This was painful. Especially as, in a few cases, these were people whose support I had been hoping for.

For my own mental health and to safeguard my recovery, I had to limit my time in those relationships.

Thankfully, the majority of people responded to my vulnerability with their own honesty. More often than not I found friends were not appalled or shocked, but responded with their own 'me too' stories.

The muscle of vulnerability has to be exercised and strengthened. It can take time in a relationship to move from feeling dangerously over-exposed to securely connected, but the reward is knowing you are accepted for who you really are.

You are seen and known and loved.

True connection is holy.
It requires a level of mask-off, skin-off vulnerability that can feel uncomfortable and unfamiliar.

I am a work-in-progress.
We are a work-in-progress.

Vulnerability is still a choice, but one I make more easily, most of the time.

The risk is worth it.

Dear Matt

In those years, as I moved further away from you, there was still a part of me that always knew this wasn't the way through. I didn't want to become contained, controlled. I wanted to be the person you fell in love with, who wore dungarees and said outrageous things. Who had energy to spare and took risks. Who loved to read and paint and sing and believed life was beautiful. And yet here I was managing my emotions, trying to ration my energy so I didn't collapse.

We had established ourselves on separate islands of survival and I didn't know how to get back to you. I couldn't think about the hard work it would take, how I would have to learn to be vulnerable with you, one painstaking footstep at a time. The idea was terrifying. If you knew how I really felt and then, reasonably, chose to reject me, what then? For a long time it was too scary to try. Safer to occasionally wave from my island to yours, keeping you at a safe distance.

But you didn't let that happen.
Somehow you remembered the me I used to be.
And when we started to risk conversation and movement, although it was hard and scary, it felt good, it felt right.

Do you remember that January when I told you to expect we would fight more that coming year?

I knew if I was going to be honest with you I needed to learn to stand my ground when we fought, to not acquiesce and always apologise first. I needed to learn to articulate how I felt, to ask for what I wanted. To see this was neither selfish or unreasonable. For so long my priority had been to restore the status quo fast while enjoying the superiority I felt from acting like 'the bigger person'. I told myself this ability to forgive quickly meant I cared about our relationship more.

It didn't.

It only revealed how hard I found it to sit in the uncomfortable space conflict created.

This is what it is taking to build a marriage of equals: to be willing to sit in the pain longer than I want. I knew I was not going to learn to advocate for myself if I didn't practise. Acting differently was destabilising. My previous approach left me feeling equal parts worthless and self-righteous, but at least I knew it worked. It made sure the row was consigned to the past in the shortest time possible. Sitting with the pain was harder but it was necessary if we were to find each other again.

And of course, you know of all the things I haven't written in these pages. All the relational pain and bereavement and disappointment that crowded in on us in the time I was ill. You know how much is unsaid. How much more has happened. I am the one here writing about my mental illness but you have suffered too my sweet. You have big shoulders and have carried so much for me, for us.

But you don't have to carry it all any more. I have been getting well for myself, but also for you, for us. We are able to carry things together now. Sometimes we are more pantomime horse than stallion, but together, we are getting there.

W IS FOR THE WALK

I meet him at the door. As he returns, I leave. The kids are fed and in their pyjamas. I figure he doesn't have to do much, just read some stories, and give the youngest his milk.

And I am out.   I am free.

   Walking down the road, trainers on, headphones in.

I cross a busy road, and meander down the path that runs by the side of a high school – the high school I once attended (and hated). I look at the yard where I endured countless breaks and lunch times and hockey and tennis. No more. The local park dates back to the Victorian era. It has seen better days but is being restored slowly, starting with the large glass building, the Palm House. The lake at its centre is being dredged and will in time see ducks and birds nesting on its banks again. For now it is grey and unexciting.

It is January. I circumnavigate the park on a path used by cyclists and runners. Occasionally I try and join their ranks, but I am a better walker than runner. I listen to the Women's Hour podcast or music or nothing. It is late winter when I start walking and, as I walk, I watch the seasons change. I feel the hard ground soften.

I watch the birds collect material for nests. I see the first buds, then the first blossom. Daffodils and crocuses appear, splashes of colour that look like hope. As the seasons change, so do I. I am walking away from my despair, my anxiety. Or trying to. I am following the seasons, looking for new life.

The following year we move house and I replace the park with the river. I'm still fighting anxiety daily, trying to stay afloat. Most days I walk in the early evening with a friend who lives locally. We aren't ambling, we are walking with purpose. Striding. Putting distance between ourselves and the day. As we walk we talk, or we are silent. We discuss the important things and the nonsense. We feel the fresh air on our skin and notice how the river looks; whether it is grey and still, or golden, reflecting a sunset, or murky under mist. The exercise helps regulate the over-production of adrenalin my anxiety causes. It encourages calm. With company I am shaking off the isolation. I am learning to be honest.

As I walk I gain perspective.
As I walk I think.

About five years ago as I walked I had an apparition, a vision. I saw God.

Not what I was expecting, and I know, impossible. But just because something didn't physically happen doesn't mean it wasn't real.

Up ahead I saw the God I had followed all of my life. I was surprised. He stood before me, waiting.

And I made a decision to walk away from him.
The God I knew had asked more than I was able to give.

He had kept me trapped in childish thinking. He hadn't let me grow up and ask questions and make decisions. I knew if I carried on following him I would become ill again.

It was with sadness I decided I could follow him no longer. I turned and walked away. Literally. I altered my path, as though he was really up ahead.

As I did, I thought I saw a man sat on the low wall that ran along the path a few yards ahead of me.
The man on the wall was Jesus.
Sometimes the truest things are impossible.
He saw me and I don't know whether it was with a roll of his eyes, or an over-the-top sigh that he said, "finally".
Turns out I'd been following the wrong guy.
The God I had been following had set expectations that were unreasonable. I knew Jesus-on-the-wall wasn't going to do that. Maybe I could still believe and be well.
I would have to wait and see.

I walk to sort out my confusion.
I walk to unravel the knots my mind has created.
I walk to feel grounded.
I walk to get my body moving and find perspective.
I walk because I enjoy it.
I walk to talk to the God I now find in the clouds and the trees and the river and in me.

is for X
Marks the Spot

Ann Voskamp's memoir is at times so dense I have to read a page three times before I can access her voice and penetrate her meaning. At other times I hear her voice clearly. She articulates truths I've been struggling to find words for. The pressure, the expectation; the life I'd been attempting to live, which was too much and never enough.

Something I read resonates with me and everything falls into place. I've been climbing. Scaling one ladder after another. Ladders of career, looking for success and acceptance in my work. The ladder which would enable me to be the mum I always felt I should be. Ladders in the church, looking for recognition; to be seen as wise, or humble, or something.

A few years into recovery finds me lying on my stomach in the early evening in a meadow in Anglesey. A welcome quiet moment. I have a bottle of beer by my side and every few minutes I prop myself up on my elbow to take a swig. The sun is hazy and the long grass tickles my bare ankles. I can hear my husband putting the kids to bed in the house nearby. They are happy and tired after a day at the beach. Sun-kissed and sandy-toed. I am reading.

The ladder of popularity, where I look right and am dynamic and throw the best parties.
Ladders everywhere when, as she writes, it is "the joy of small that makes life large." [3]

I've been climbing, thinking that if I could just get a little further I would have made it.
But to where?

And I remember my friend Frank on the radio. He said to see the world – to really live – you only have to stand still. To pay attention. [4]

And there and then, in that field, surrounded by sky and long grass and buzzing insects I decide: no more.
No more ladders. No more climbing. No more trying to reach... what? I don't even know.

Here.
I like it here.

I will find a way to be okay, here, now.
In this moment.

I remember the decision.

A pulling of the metaphorical, down into the dust and the dirt, to determine the way I would now live.

I want to be present.
I want to pay attention and see the good.
I don't want to miss anything by looking forward to how things could be or back with regret at how things had been.
I want to find joy in the day-to-day messy reality of my life.
No more climbing ladders.
I will stay on the ground in the garden and make it as beautiful as I can.

Ann Voskamp:
"This is what it means to fully live." [5]

3. p.167 from *1000 Gifts*; Ann Voskamp
4. *Desert Island Discs* with Frank Cottrell-Boyce, first broadcast, 26 March 2010. www.bbc.co.uk
5. p.226 from *1000 Gifts*; Ann Voskamp

How to stay married for 18 years

1

Keep talking. When you need space and time to think, take it, but come back together and keep the conversation going, don't pretend it never happened.

2

Remember your family is not their family. Sometimes you will see them together but it's also ok to let your partner off the hook and take the kids to see your parents without them (and for them to do the same for you!).

3

Try and understand where each other is coming from. If appropriate and possible talk to their therapist to find out how you can help them.

4

Look after yourself. Don't expect anyone else to and don't spend all your time caring for others.

5

Take it in turns to have a lie in.

6

Be prepared to hear things you don't want to hear. If you are going to learn how to be vulnerable with each other this is an inevitable side effect. Try and listen without judgement or taking it too personally. Take a deep breath before you respond.

7

Never underestimate the benefit of couples therapy. Marriage is hard, it's okay to need help.

8

Share your hopes and expectations. There is nothing more likely to cause unnecessary conflict than misaligned expectations; what you will do on the weekend, if you'll attend that bbq, or how much you'll spend on a wedding present.

9

And while we're on money, discuss it, often. Talk about your separate contributions to the family, whether that is time or service or financial – they all cost you to give, just because one of you earns less doesn't mean they are offering less.

10

Do Christmas your way. Be with family or be alone. Set your own traditions and don't be afraid to tell your extended family how you will be doing it. Make a plan together and don't apologise for it.

11

Don't make the mistake of thinking your happiness is your partner's responsibility. It isn't, it's yours. Figure out how to pursue it.

12

Keep all your important documents, including passports in a safe place, it will save you frantic stressful evenings together.

13

Talk about sex. Even if it feels awkward and complicated. In fact, especially then.

14

Never have sex out of duty.

15

Invest in good friends. Find people who you can laugh with, be silly with, and cry with. You will need them all.

16

Express gratitude to each other. Or I could say, don't take each other for granted.

17

Go to bed at the same time, often.

18

Recognise the season you are in, if it is time to work hard and keep your head down, talk about how you will handle that. If it is time to rest keep each other accountable to make sure you get it.

Y is for Yellow Dress

It arrived
in a parcel with numerous
other pieces of clothing.
All brightly-coloured items,
but this one stood out.
A yellow dress.
Sunshine yellow.
Short and summery.

I wouldn't have dreamt of wearing something like this a few short years ago. Back when my wardrobe was almost entirely navy or black. When I chose clothes with the sole aim of finding things that made me look thinner. When I wore clothes hoping they would show less of me: less thigh, less untoned arm, less postpartum soft stomach.

I didn't obsess about how I looked, but I would never have said I loved my body. It was okay, so long as I didn't draw too much attention to it. If it wasn't noticed too often.

But, as I've leant into the joy of accepting all the parts of me, I've found a desire to accept the flesh and bones that surround the soul and mind and spirit I've been attending to.

As I've become braver, I've started to pull the unspoken anxieties about how I look into the light of day, to look my insecurities in the eye and expose the quiet voice that whispers to me: 'I would look better and be worth more if I was thinner. I would be liked more and feel more successful if I lost weight.'

I'm calling this what it is: a lie.

A distraction from the important things in life.
And if this feeling of not measuring up is a lie, I've started asking, what is the truth?

I know you can't replace a lie with a vacuum — it doesn't work. You have to replace a lie with something else. The truth seems like a good place to start.

Here it is. (Brace yourselves.)

My body is magnificent.
(And so is yours.)
I have strong arms that have rocked babies to sleep. I have a back that has transported children up and down the stairs. I have eyes that can see the beauty of this season of the year. I have ears that can hear music and a mouth that can taste food. I have hands that can dig the earth, and braid my girls' hair, and clean the bathroom and type these words.

My body is not disgusting, or 'too much'. It is beautiful.

There is beauty in the actions it performs. And (I say, while blowing a raspberry at shame), there is beauty in the way my body looks. There is beauty in the design. It feels dangerous to say that I am beautiful.
To love myself enough.

To not censor myself through fear of how you will read this. But I will say it. I am beautiful.
It is a truth I am learning to claim because this beauty is not in short supply. This is not a competition. I am beautiful and you are beautiful. From the colour of your eyes to the breadth of my smile. Beauty does not need to be viewed from the position of scarcity.

Beauty is everywhere.

And, while I'm on a roll of truth-telling, I'll tell you what else I know when I stop being distracted by the nonsense: the magazines and the internet and drip-drip-drip that values youth and unattainable weight goals and flawless skin and symmetrical features and models who pose with their mouths open like they're catching flies.

Beauty is not about dress size, or complexion, it's not about fashion or age. Beauty is about the heart. Like the kids song we used to sing, it's what's in the heart that counts. Beauty abounds where there is kindness and acceptance. Beauty is found where there is trust and a willingness to be vulnerable.

Beauty is about love.
Knowing you are loved and loving others.
Risking love.
Even loving yourself.
Especially loving yourself.

Any time I find myself caught in a moment of longing for the size 8 bodies of my sisters, I'm reminded that my body is just perfect as it is.

I open my wardrobe and take out the yellow dress.

"All shall be well, and all shall be well and all manner of thing shall be well."— **Lady Julian of Norwich**

For a long time I thought healing was the answer to the question my illness asked. Illness was a sign something was badly wrong in my soul or heart or the world, right?

I spent a long time waiting for the happy ending, when I would stand and say I was now better. That my mental health was inviolable. When I would proclaim the trial was over and I was through the storm.
(I know all the metaphors.)

There have been many times when I wished this was the case. I've known my fair share of nights, desperate and pleading, while anxiety prowled and consumed me.

But I have not been healed, and most of the time now, I am not waiting to be.

is for

Impossible

Zero

I am accepting of this new me.

Complicated.
Vulnerable.
Raw.
(Brilliant).

Of course, this is easier for me to say today, with over a year of good health where I've only experienced relatively minor skirmishes with my mental illness.

It is easier for me to accept my frailty when it is not defining my life. Ask me again when I wake with my heart pounding, finding myself spiralling into the abyss. I might think differently. (I never claimed to be consistent.) Accepting my un-healing has been a process. A gradual dawning. Because there has been no overnight success story, I have had to learn to manage my mental health. This has taken time and effort.

I have refined the recipe to enable me to live well. It constantly evolves but at present consists of (among other things): long walks, being outdoors, lowering my expectations, doing less, and the antidepressant I take every morning.

If I had been healed, I wouldn't have learnt to understand and care for my body and mind. I wouldn't have seen the beautiful necessity of self-compassion. I wouldn't have taken responsibility for myself and made a decision to curate my own life. But I have learnt and changed and it has been the most joyous and freeing experience.

If I had been healed I wouldn't have become the me I am now, who I really like.

I am a completely different person to who I was ten years ago. Learning how to live again has changed almost everything about me. My relationships are more honest, my marriage is stronger and my kids have a mum who is able to be open with them. I have discovered my life is richer with complexity than without it.

I haven't been healed, because my un-healing tells a better story than my healing could have.

When you appear you've got it all together, when this is the persona you give to those around you, it's hard for them to connect with you.

Anything too shiny, too slippery, is hard to attach to.
As I have learnt to live open and broken it has become easier for others to belong to me, and me to belong to them.
With my inside on the outside, I live fully as myself.

I am not numbed but alive, present. Aware.
I am not sleepwalking.
I am not on autopilot.
I am more fragile than I used to be, but it is not damaging any more, it has become my strength.

It is a fire on a hill top.
A bonfire visible across the valley, way out to the coast.

Finally

And, breathe.

These days, I enjoy life.
I make plans. I eat in restaurants. I book holidays.

Things that felt impossible a few years ago have become part of my everyday life.

I enjoy my work and can concentrate for longer stretches.
I read.

Life has opened up.

I will not go back to faster and bigger and better and more.
I will not go back to good.
I have found a better way to be: present.
On this mission to find relief, that is what I have learnt:

Accept the day as it unfolds.
Life is big and complicated and you can't control it.
Celebrate the successes and have grace for when the
travelator you've been moving along appears to take you
back to somewhere you've already been.
Be patient with your flesh and blood.

Don't despise your fragility and slow recovery.
You will have good and bad days. Days when you feel you
can do everything and days when it's a battle to get out of
bed.

It is okay.

Remember the present moment of anxiety will lessen, the
panic will dial down, you will know peace and calm, you
will laugh and feel joy again.

Take a moment.

Take a breath.

Relax your shoulders. There is no rush.

You are enough as you are, in this minute, without doing or
saying or being anything other than exactly as you are.

Thank you

Matt, for everything.

To my wonderful kids, for making me laugh and keeping me on my toes. I adore you.

Amanda, for pointing out the darkness and lighting the way out.

Sri, Marita, Sally and Katie, for reading my words along the way; for your input, wisdom and generosity.

Jan, for always being there.
Laura, for the Bat-Signals and the story about the hippo.
Sri, for inspiring and loving me.

To fellow travellers and friends:
Tim, Alistair, Kerry, Mark and Penny, Mark and Jo.
 We need a reunion.

To Fiona, editor extraordinaire, for making me sound good.